"Unlocking Legacy is a j ... a journey of intercessory prayer, but also for those who have walked it long. It is not so much about strategy and formula as it is about intimacy and obedience.

This book offers stories of ordinary people pursuing God's will in specific circumstances and seeing Him do what he has asked them to pray for. Our qualifications are intimacy and obedience to the Author and Finisher of our faith, Jesus Christ!"
–Rev. Jeff Frost, Campus Pastor, Prayer Track Leader, Eston College

Much of our prayer journey unfolds in that secret place of relationship between us and God—effectively hiding many of its more intimate aspects. *Unlocking Legacy* provides snapshots of these more personal moments, allowing us to be a quiet observer. Being a witness to these affectionate exchanges **expands our understanding** of the capacity in which we can walk and talk with God. Reading this heart-felt book is a life changing experience.
Jocelyn A. Drozda, Author of *Ancient Paths: Unraveling the Mystery of Divine Guidance* and *Invisible No More: Personal Identity Restored*

"Oh my dear gracious and loving heavenly Father, how can I not praise You for your faithfulness in raising up an army of warriors in today's world? . . . Thank You for giving MaryAnn the stamina, discernment and ability to find and record what You have done. Thank You for the wisdom she has in sharing with us the many facets of prayer. **Thank You for the encouragement this book has given me to keep on, to be bolder, to trust You more and to not worry about the 'what if's.'** You are in control! I bless You, Jesus, and honor You for MaryAnn and this book. May You use it extensively to bless and teach others about prayer. In Jesus' name I pray. Amen."
–Sheldina Brunner, Missionary, SIM,

"**Eloquently written** teaching on prayer that is backed by the Word of God and filled with the perspectives and testimonies of many brothers and sisters in Christ."
–Megan Mvoula

"I appreciated reading your book so much... How blessed I was! I found I was not able to rush—meditating on each chapter, taking it in slowly, trying to apply it to my life. I appreciated the multifaceted approach to prayer. Although I have experienced or heard of each of these prayer forms, I'm sure I have never seen them all together before, and each one lends strength to the others.

The chapter I found most inspiring was chapter six, about creative worship movement. I am a very creative person but had not thought of the things I do and create as prayer. I also enjoyed thinking about prophetic acts, beyond those seen in scripture."
– Rhonda Bagwell

"MaryAnn uses vivid and striking imagery to paint a picture of what a journey in prayer looks like. This book inspired me in my prayer life and legacy. The depth and richness of communing with God is so amazing and precious here and now . . . a glimpse of what it will be when we are 'home.' "
– Tina Maki

"Prayer has become an increasingly important part of my walk with God, but while reading *Unlocking Legacy* by MaryAnn Ward, God began to challenge me more and more to put my feet to my prayers. The stories shared throughout the book, especially Chapter 11 "The Help God Sends" and Chapter 12 "The Power of Testimony," caused my heart to beat faster and the tears to flow. I was convicted of fear of man and fear of failure, and inspired to accept the challenge, as one of the voices in the book stated, "to be the answer to prayer by one act of obedience at a time." I believe God will use what I've read to propel me into new territory in the upcoming days, weeks and months. A key message throughout the book is the compassion of the Father's heart . . . Another quote which struck a chord with me was "I cannot walk in compassion without feeling enough, being angry enough, fervent enough to go past my 'chicken line' to make a difference in the lives of others." *Unlocking Legacy* is a beautifully written tapestry of the many facets of prayer, as unique as each individual's relationship with our Creator. It was both pleasurable and impactful and I believe it will make a difference in every reader's life.
– Michele Hastings

UNLOCKING LEGACY

Taking Your God-given Territory Through Prayer

MaryAnn Ward

Copyright

Publisher's Cataloging-in-Publication Date

Names: Ward, MaryAnn, author.
Title: Unlocking legacy : taking your God-given territory through prayer / MaryAnn Ward.
Description: Balgonie, SK : ReMade Ministries, 2020. Summary: Offers practical illustrations concerning how to possess what God has already made available to us through prayer. Powerful, personal encounters with God in prayer demonstrate how ordinary people pray with authority, claiming their God-given inheritance.
Identifiers: ISBN 9781777130046 (pbk.) | ISBN 9781777130053 (hard cover) | ISBN 97817771300604 (ebook) | ISBN 9781777130077 (audio)
Subjects: LCSH: Christian life. | Spiritual life – Christianity. | Prayer – Christianity. | BISAC: RELIGION /Christian Living / Prayer. | RELI GION / Christian Living / Spiritual Growth. | RELIGION / Prayer.
Classification: LCC BV220 W37 | DDC 248.32--dc23

Published and Printed in Canada by
ReMade Ministries
Box 205, Balgonie, SK S0G 0E0

Dedication

To the forerunners who carried the mantle of
prayer with integrity and passion,
and now, in trust, passed it
to our generation.
Thank you.

Table of Contents

Introduction

Boot camp has ended. Orders for deployment have arrived, sending prayer warriors to the front lines—equipped and ready to take on the adversary.

Regardless of the victory already won through Jesus Christ, the enemy continues to intimidate and mock. Sometimes he comes with guerilla warfare, sneaking up from behind, picking off the unsuspecting, idle and weak. At other times, the attack is frontal and fierce.

Unlocking Legacy draws wisdom from dozens of war savvy veterans of all ages. They share their experiences and expertise so that every prayer warrior and intercessor will be encouraged and inspired to *"take possession of the land."* As you listen to their stories, may you glean from their insights!

> **"See, I have given you this land. Go in and take**
> **possession of the land the LORD swore he would**
> **give to your fathers — to Abraham, Isaac and Jacob**
> **— and to their descendants after them."**
> **Deuteronomy 1:8**

The moment by moment, battle by battle, strategies come directly from our Commander and Chief, Jesus Christ. The enemy has no new tactics, relying on fear and lies to deflate and defeat God's army. He would like to confine us to a prison for which he no longer holds the keys. No more!

The keys are in the hand of our Victor,

> **"I am the Living One; I was dead, and now look, I**
> **am alive for ever and ever! And I hold the**
> **keys of death and Hades."**
> **Revelation 1:18**

Isaiah declared Jesus would possess the keys and **"what he opens no one can shut, and what he shuts no one can open"** (Is 22:22). Later, Jesus said to His followers, **"I will give you the keys of the kingdom of heaven; whatever you bind on earth will be bound in heaven, and whatever you loose on earth will be loosed in heaven"** (Mt 16:19). We have been given keys, mighty keys, to unlock and unleash the dynamic power and unconditional love of God through prayer.

Even though God declares the territory is already ours, we must seize and secure our inheritance through spiritual warfare. He is with us every step of the way, as we take our rightful possession back from the world, the flesh and the devil.

With each key, we have authority to unlock our God-given legacy waiting for us, revealing personal and corporate destiny.

***

"Only through intimacy with the Father, Jesus Christ and Holy Spirit will we know what God really wants to do through prayer."
– Mark

***

"I had to learn authority. I had to learn the Word. I had to learn travail. I had to learn how to hear prophetically. Then I had to learn to put it all together and let God govern."
– Charlene

***

"With every healing I see, every salvation I witness, every deliverance that happens, I'm making satan pay."
– Emmanuel

CHAPTER 1

Come in Low
– Humility

> *"I am only twenty-one years old, not amazing or academically smart. The way the Lord uses me is all from Him."*
> *– Caleb*

We walked together through the graveyard of distant memory dotted with tombstones of prayers unanswered. I'm the reluctant follower and He the patient Guide. As if it were only yesterday, I hear again my desperate cries for rescue from pain and pleas for life restored to one too young to die—prayers first declared with fists clenched, then spoken from knees bent, and finally whispered faintly with head bowed.

"Why? Why must I remember?" My throat tightens in the futile attempt to suppress emotion from spewing its ugly bile, piercing the paper-thin veil of denial.

Through the cemetery He leads, stopping briefly to face each marker. Brushing debris from carefully etched inscriptions, He reveals succinct details of each prayer initiative. As we walk, He holds my hand firmly in His, bringing comfort as ancient wounds are exposed—naked, stripped and bare. Only with Him, would I dare venture into these frigid shadows. Questions turn into indisputable answers as we walk together.

From dawn's first appearing until the sun's full rise, He tenderly led the way, penetrating the healing oil of revelation into each memory. Gradually, the patterns of my frail prayer journey take form.

Each stone marker signified a close relative, loved too deeply and held too long.

Aunt Arrogance and Uncle Unbelief,

Junior Judgment and Cousin Critical,

Brother Bitterness and Daughter Doubt,

lying next to Sister Sin.

For me, though not for Him, the graveyard tour seemed long—sapping strength, denying hope and magnifying loss. I breathed a deep sigh of relief as we passed through the open gate toward a narrow path which angled sharply to the right as it edged upward. All the while, He adjusted to my slower pace, never leaving my side.

Upon reaching a small summit, we sat quietly together—hearts still and knowing. With spring long gone and summer reluctantly giving way to fall, the heavy scent of harvest filled the air with the promise of labor's reward. From this elevation, the tombstones looked more like milestones saluting the progress of developed prayer. Each stone, rather than marking the place of failure, pointed onlookers toward a large wooden cross upon which He, the One who still held my hand, once hung.

Prayers tainted by the rawness of emotion and the brokenness of my human heart had to die. Only those humbly voiced in surrender to the Lord's perfect will held the continuum of life. In the shadow of the cross

proud petitions are silenced,

the foolish angst of childhood stilled,

selfish desires quenched, and

retaliation for offense nullified.

He turned my gaze from the dismal landscape below to the cerulean blue sky. With unmoving wings, eagles soared effortlessly upward. They rose ever higher, circling on currents of warm surrender until they touched the clouds.

With unspoken words, God helped me understand that through humility, by coming in low, He carries prayer high. Entering into His Presence in prayer can never be arrogant, but it must be bold.

Suddenly, with brazen interruption the accuser appeared, pointing back to the graveyard of unanswered prayer. He taunted, "You? You are too sinful to approach the Father. He won't, can't and refuses to hear your prayers now." His words slurred and stretched with disdain, echoing my fear and regret, as I hung my head in shame-filled resignation.

His words though right were deadly wrong.

Jesus squeezed my hand gently, then rose victoriously to His feet, taking His stand between me and my accuser. "Not true!" His voice boomed with authority, thundering through the hills, resonating past time for all Heaven and hell to hear.

"Preposterous!" the adversary seethed. "Clearly she is too weak and flawed to pray again."

"Forgiven!" He spoke not to the accuser, but to me. With a single word, the judgment was rendered, sending the adversary slithering back into the dark dungeon from which he came.

Jesus refocused my attention to an adjacent hillside where a festive celebration was assembling. Throngs of people gathered in excitement—their joy contagious and inviting.

"What's happening?" I asked. "Is it a wedding? A family reunion, perhaps?"

Together we watched as the crowd cascaded over the brim of the hill like froth overflowing a glass. They approached with exuberance—laughing, dancing and praising God.

These were
>> once prisoners in chains but now free,
>> once blind but now received their sight,
>> once persecuted but now exonerated,
>> once prodigals but now safely returned home
> —the redeemed, children of God.

Jesus embraced each one, ruffling the hair of some, high-fiving others, tenderly embracing yet more, sharing and amplifying their joy. Then one-by-one they came to me. Shaking my hand, they looked beyond my eyes into the depth of my heart. "Thank you for praying," they said.

Unbelieving, I glanced over my shoulder at the graveyard, then back to the multitude and finally to Him. **"With man it is impossible, but with God all things are possible"** (Mt 19:26). The pain of failure held no comparison to the joy of triumph. Humbled by God's favor, I knew more than ever that in Him alone every victory was won. My only qualification to enter the place of prayer reads, **". . . in Christ Jesus you who once were far off have been brought near by the blood of Christ"** (Eph 2:13).

No expiry date mars prayer's open invitation. Nothing diminishes prayer's essence of wonder. The key that opens the door of prayer is clearly labeled "humility". With it, we enter the throne room of God to petition, linger and listen—ready to obey.

Though Jesus walks with us through the cemetery of unanswered prayer, He never abandons us there. He takes us onward to view the cross, to catch the wisp of harvest, and to see the reward of fervent trust. With an awareness of His undeserved grace and an attitude of reverent humility, He invites us to come again and again in prayer, laying our requests before Him where

His silence is sweet,

His voice fierce,

His arms inviting,

His majesty overwhelming,

His power sufficient,

His authority indisputable.

For that reason, we continue to pray.

Personal Perspectives

In conversation with Merodee, she said,

"Over and over in our prayer journey, we have the answers and the seemingly unanswered. In everything profitable, there

4

is one big decision supported by a hundred other decisions. Every day and many times throughout the day, we continue to draw near to God.

"I had a dream in which I was pregnant and in labor. The doctor came and said there wasn't one baby but two. With joy I moved to the floor, rocking and weeping, 'Thank You, Lord. We have asked for one and You have given us two.'

"When I woke up, I sensed God was talking about two ministries. I knew that I had to birth one and the other would come. It was one work. I realized the twins in my dream were kings and priests who represented God to the people. As they made themselves available, God gave them an opportunity. With opportunity came boldness and opposition. If we would travail in prayer, laboring as priests, the birth of the kingly ministry would follow.

> **"While they were worshiping as priests before the
> Lord in prayer and fasting, the Holy Spirit said,
> 'I have called Barnabas and Saul to do an
> important work for me. Now, release them
> to go and fulfill it.' So, after they had fasted
> and prayed, they laid hands on them
> and sent them off."**
> **Acts 13:2-3 TPT**

"God asked, 'You have the desire for ministry, but are you available?'

Whatever is asked of me is provided for me.

" 'Teach me to pray Lord,' is our request. He does so much more, pouring out the spirit of travail, inviting us to draw near to Him. In prayer, I must remain small, resisting the temptation to pull away and allowing the conviction of Holy Spirit to draw near, compelling me to fast and worship. My righteousness is in Christ alone. If we remain small there is so much God can do.

"It is the humility of prayer,
    being emptied of what we want,
        sitting quietly in His Presence,
            letting the Spirit of prayer use us, that
                is profoundly overwhelming.

"We daily have the invitation in the prayer closet to ask, 'Lord, give me the words.' When we come as an open empty vessel through which the Holy Spirit can flow, He won't be far. Then we will know Jesus' glory flow through us in prayer, seeing His beauty, understanding His heart, and beholding Him not from afar but from within. Here His peace guards our hearts and minds in Christ Jesus (Phil 4:7). We aren't to be looking ahead to a kingly calling but to remain small and humble in prayer, birthing what God desires.

"In prayer, there is the chaos of childhood—responsive or reactionary. Then there is the disciplinary prayer that brings order and puts structures in place. Finally, there is a lifestyle of prayer, mature and unceasing, blending adoration and supplication. Each stage is beautiful and precious.

"Daniel couldn't bow before King Nebuchadnezzar because his heart was already bowed in complete humility to another greater King, the Lord God (Dn 3). To obtain a Daniel-like resolve, it's not the strength to stand in the face of opposition we must possess, but rather the strength to bend before the Lord in humility.

"Daniel **'got down on his knees and prayed, giving thanks to his God'** morning, noon and evening (Dn 6:10). Jesus also slipped away to pray in the morning, sent His disciples away at noon to solitary places, and sought out time with His Father at night. The lifestyle of prayer has a rhythm of inviting us back to humility—bending and bowing before our Lord.

"I read in our church history, 'We didn't have to decide to pray.

Prayer came upon us.' When we make ourselves available for prayer and humble ourselves under it, prayer *comes*. The continuum of prayer—childlikeness, discipline, and lifestyle—brings us to the place of laying ourselves down saying, 'Holy Spirit, have Your way.' We come in low and humble. Then we let God breathe His strategy of prayer into our lives.

> *I desired a praying lifestyle, but I didn't know it would come at the price of humility.*

"There is something in me that wants to turn prayer into a work. I can be tempted to believe that the answers are a by-product of my own doing. Everything God offers is a gift of grace, including prayer. I pray that there would be a heaviness that settles on me to respond to God in prayer."

Joy-Lyn says,

"Prayer carried a lot of guilt for me when I felt like I should be praying for people but wasn't. Then the Holy Spirit challenged me, 'Praying for someone out of guilt is just as bad as not praying for someone I told you to pray for.' I saw praying for others as an obedience thing.

"There were times I chose to listen to the Holy Spirit's voice and obeyed. There were also times I sensed God's prompts and didn't follow through. I had to realize that praying and answers to prayer are all because of Jesus. It is *all* Jesus!

"When I was younger, I had an understanding that prayer was the right thing to do. I never explored or evaluated why. As I grew older, in my early teens, I saw the alternatives and choices people were making and the results in their lives. Then I knew for sure that Jesus was the right way to live my life. Finally, I came to a point where praying and reading my Bible were out of pure desperation, knowing that if I didn't, I would have nothing else. When I was seventeen, I started spending time in prayer and Bible reading because I needed to, not just because I wanted to. I couldn't get through my day if I didn't, or at least my day wouldn't turn out well. More and more I positioned myself in a place of humility before God.

"I grew up watching my parents' worship, raising their hands and singing with all their hearts. I would go to church not feeling like worshiping at all. I spent about three years not engaging in worship and not understanding what I was missing while waiting for a moment or an encounter.

"My Dad told me, 'We don't worship because we feel something, we worship because the Lord is worthy. We worship because that is what we are meant to do.'

"I have never looked back. Whether I feel like it or not, I passionately worship the Lord. Out of worship the encounters, the moments, come. Worship is the one thing I have to give the Lord that He doesn't already have.

"Worship and prayer aren't something I do when I go to church. Worship and prayer are acts of submission of my spirit to the Lord. Worship and prayer are Holy Spirit led, allowing Him to steer me in any direction. By His prompting, in humility, I worship Him and pray for people and things."

Kate said,

"Humbly, we cast all our crowns at His feet. Anything that is of God in my life, originates from Him. It has nothing to do with me. He gets all the thanksgiving and the glory for everything godly that comes out of my life.

"There is a continuation of the awe of the Lord and a deepening reverence for Him. In prayer, we come in awe of His sovereignty, knowing that all the glory and praise goes to Him.

"God calls me to simply show up in prayer, yielding myself in obedience. True prayer is His ministry through us. To communicate with Almighty God is incredible. Knowing He wants to have fellowship with us is very humbling. Prayer is the ultimate communication to have."

In our interview, Emily also commented on humility.

"Be humble and stay humble! In the whole process, never run ahead of the Lord. He is your Master. Yes, pray and utilize your spiritual gifts, however, be humble before God and have respect for all people. Humility is the process God uses for Him to be able to use us.

"When I was young, my head was always up in the sky. God has brought me down so low. Since I was sixteen, I've had a hunger and grace for prayer that has come from Him alone, but He had yet to bring me through the process of humility. Humility is a daily surrendering, where our flesh is pruned away so Christ can be formed. Humility is necessary to know who He made me to be in Christ and what He has planned for me.

"In the hard places, God brings one to realize that everything one needs is in Him. I have everything I need because He has given me Himself; Christ is my inheritance. I'm so thankful."

Two years ago, a friend and I visited a dear gentle saint in the hospital. She had extensive open sores on her lower legs which her diabetic body was unable to heal. Without the amputation of her legs, the surgeons gave her two weeks to live. She was more willing to turn from Earth's struggles to Heaven's glory than to consent to the radical surgery. When we prayed for her complete healing, she experienced an intense warm feeling in the diseased part of her legs, but there were no visible changes to her condition.

This beautiful woman slowly recovered. Over the past two years, I have visited her several times. I'm always challenged by her complete humility and passionate love for her Savior and others. Thankfulness, rather than criticism, constantly flows from this beautiful woman.

Did our prayers make a difference in her healing? Beyond a doubt! Were our prayers the turning point? Maybe, maybe not!

Dozens of people had been praying and continue to pray for her. Every single petition on her behalf moved the hand of God. My friend and I simply were a part of the greater crowd of witnesses, aligning ourselves together on her behalf.

Meekness and humility recognize humanity's smallness in light of God's greatness. Even in those times when instant and dramatic healing occurs, we err if we boast in ourselves as if we brought about some great thing. Prayer allows God to speak His intension through us. **"Let the one who boasts boast in the Lord"** (1 Cor 1:31).

Allison shared with me her understanding of the connection between humility and prayer.

"I have witnessed arrogance and pride in the prayer world, both in me and in others. People sometimes assume they have specialized knowledge or revelation about prayer, creating inaccessibility to prayer for all Christians. Yes, God can give revelation knowledge to some people, but pride lords such revelation over others, creating a stumbling block in their minds.

"Jesus reveals himself to everyone freely, inviting all believers to pray. He welcomes everyone to seek Him and empowers us all to intimately engage with Him in prayer.

10

"Some people might try to convince you to pray a specific way: 'Follow these twelve steps in prayer, but if you don't you won't see the answers.' Such fallacy creates the belief that prayer is for professionals and elite prayer specialists.

> *Humility makes prayer accessible to everyone while honoring the Gospel and the heart of God.*

"Pride creeps in so subtly that we can be ignorant of its presence. 'Do you know how much I've fasted? Do you know how many people I've seen healed?' Lack of humility may spring from insecurity, the need for personal significance or a person's desire to find their place in the body of Christ. We've all been there!

"What does humility look like? To me, it looks like surrender. When we use prayer as a means of control, in any fashion, humility is lacking. Humility possesses a soft heart toward God and faith in people's relationship with Jesus while honoring God's sovereignty. Humility holds the highest value.

"Compassion for people with chronic illnesses or praying for loved ones to come to the Lord grows as we encounter those things too. If we can reflect on our unanswered prayers, learning and allowing God to build faith in us through them, we gain compassion for others. God is no less good or His power no less real or accessible to us because we haven't seen answers to those things yet.

"However, we persist. Second Peter 1:5-7 says,

'For this reason, make every effort to add to your faith goodness; and to goodness, knowledge; and to knowledge, self-control; and to self-control, perseverance; and to perseverance, godliness; and to godliness, mutual affection; and to

mutual affection, love.'

"These are all qualities of humility in prayer.

"It's easy to have a practice of prayer based on answered prayers as opposed to the practice of prayer based on the character of God. I want to see the power of God released through prayer, and I want to know who God is even if I don't see circumstances change. That has been a wrestle for me.

"I have been humbled by living my Christian life with Christians from many different denominational backgrounds. Through those experiences, I've grown to appreciate the different ways God answers prayer and the different practices of prayer."

Unlocking the Legacy

Many people have learned through experience that
the humble are often trampled,
the meek are usually bullied,
and the weak are regularly ignored.
In our attempts to have an impact for the Kingdom of God, we have all too frequently assumed the ways of the world. Contrary to God's intention, we have resorted to self-promotion, human effort or wisdom, and the misuse of positions of influence for both good and evil.

One of the great struggles most Christians face is to completely lay aside ourselves so God, and God alone, will be glorified in everything we do, including prayer: not through a false humility which is pride in disguise, but through the awareness that **"every good and perfect"** thing comes from the Father (Jas 1:17). Jesus did it all; every victory was won through His death and resurrection.

*". . . a Lamb-turned-Lion descended into this death
camp through the porthole of Golgatha. Crashing
through the gates of hell, He met the dark prince in the
mother of all battles. With three spikes and a thorny
crown, the Captain of the Host conquered the devil,
eternally disarming his destructive weapons of sin,
death, hell and the grave."* [1]

Prayer must be void of any effort to impress God or others. Though we pray scriptural prayers in the power of the Holy Spirit, with wisdom and understanding, every answer comes through God's divine grace according to His perfect will.

We prefer formulas over fellowship and systems of prayer over the process. Jesus didn't offer His disciples the luxury of charted formulas. He invited them into an ever-deepening relationship. Even in the most quoted prayer of all time, **"Our Father . . ."** Jesus taught us that prayer is about an intimate connection with a Person—God, our Father. We approach the throne of God's grace boldly, but humbly, not as slaves but as friends of Jesus knowing the Father's desire (Jn 15:14-15).

Every time we abandon our relationship with God for a formula or personal agenda, we err in the high calling of prayer.

Every prayer Jesus prayed,
>   every miracle He performed,
>   every deliverance He orchestrated,
>   every hungry mouth He filled,
>   every funeral He turned into a living encounter,
every word He taught, flowed from an unhindered relationship with His Father—submitting to the Father's will, purpose and ways.

Meekness and humility are fraternal twins. Jesus said,

**"Blessed are the *meek*,
for they will *inherit* the earth."
Matthew 5:5**
(Emphasis mine)

God has given us the keys to unlock our legacy, taking territory and possessing our inheritance, through the blood of Jesus Christ.

To do so we must accept the posture of complete meekness and humility. In this verse, meekness is not an outward expression of emotion but an inward grace of the soul and calmness toward God. It is the acceptance of how God deals with each of us, considering it good and enhancing the closeness of our relationship with Him, including mildness and forbearance.[2]

Perhaps it broadens our understanding by knowing that meekness comes from a military term referring to horses. When wild stallions were brought down from the mountains and trained, depending on their temperament some were used for work, others for racing, but the finest were trained for war.[3]

Warhorses retained their fierce spirit, courage, and power, but were disciplined to respond to the slightest nudge of the rider. They would gallop on to the battlefield, coming to a sliding stop at a word, unfazed by the brutal sights, sounds and smells of warfare. This was considered true meekness—incredible strength and undying spirit under the complete control of another.

Jesus demonstrated humility and meekness perfectly. True strength knows when to assert itself and when to be passive, as opposed to reacting purely out of emotion. Those who walk in humility and meekness possess a strength to effectively defend themselves and what they value while knowing they are not in control. It is the attributes of humility and meekness that bring us to understand that we are simple but competent, capable and crucial instruments of the One who is.

Jesus humbled Himself and washed the disciples' feet, not because He forgot His greatness and power, but because He knew who He was, what His mission required and where He was going.

"It was just before the Passover Festival. Jesus *knew* that the hour had come for him to leave this world and go to the Father. *Having loved* his own who were in the world, he loved them to the end . . . Jesus *knew* that the Father had put all things under his power, and that he had come from God and was returning to God; so he got up from the meal, took off his outer clothing, and wrapped a towel around his waist . . . began to wash his disciples' feet, dry-

14

ing them with the towel . . .You call me 'Teacher' and
'Lord,' and rightly so, for that is what I am. Now
that I, your Lord and Teacher, have washed your
feet, you also should wash one another's feet.
I have set you an example that you should
do as I have done for you . . ."
John 13:1-17
(Emphasis mine)

The strength and power of a horse are not effective when denied. In the same way, both the strength and power of prayer flow effectively when it is yielded in humility and grace to God.

Effective prayer comes from those who know who they are and the God to whom they belong. Effective prayer flows from those who know the power they possess and the One who holds that power. Effective prayer moves in authority under the One who possesses all authority. James asserts, **"The prayer of a righeous person is powerful and effective"** (Jm 5:16).

As we focus on Christ, in relationship with the Father, we are neither blind followers nor passionless cowards. We are warhorses, led into battle—trained, instructed and submitted to the Rider's command. We cooperate with His power and authority, taking the keys of victory into hell's corridor, and setting people free from inevitable destruction and death. We yield to the soft hand of the Master, going where He directs, saying what He says and doing what He asks us to do.

In this place, pride has no room, but through meekness and humility, God's greatest desires are accomplished.

We must be both people committed to prayer, and people who love their relationship with God more than anything else. Such will be those who take the keys, unlocking legacy and doing great exploits for the One they know and love (Dn 11:32).

**"If my people, who are called by my name,
will *humble* themselves and pray and seek my face
and turn from their wicked ways, then I will hear
from Heaven, and I will forgive their sin and
will heal their land. Now *my eyes* will
be *open* and *my ears attentive* to the**

prayers offered in this place."
2 Chronicles 7:14-15
(Emphasis mine)

Taking Territory

"Father we come today, refusing to deny the power and greatness of who You are or the greatness of what You have called us to do in prayer. We accept the key of humility as a strategic tool You have given us for unlocking the legacy You have for both us and others.

"Jesus, You said, **'whoever believes in me will do the works I have been doing, and they will do even greater things than these'** (Jn 14:12). Because of the finished work of the cross, we yield ourselves completely to Your authority and sovereign will. We are not satisfied with what we have already seen You accomplish; we ask for greater. Like war horses fully submitted to our Rider, we come in prayer, running into the battlefield on Your behalf, unafraid of the arrows, spears and flaming torches coming from the enemy camp. We come in prayer to **'do even greater things than these.'** Give us a fresh understanding and a tenacity in prayer to pursue greater and greater miracles of Your grace.

"May the unanswered prayers of the past not in any way diminish our faith. What You did for others, do again, Lord. We want to see Your hand at work in our time. As war horses, meek and humble, with a fierce spirit and courageous tenacity, we are yielded instruments, trained for Your purposes, releasing the power of prayer.

"We throw aside the cloak of pride that would deny Your greatness and the crown of false humility which diminishes both who You've called us to be and the great things You have called us to do for Your Kingdom. We secure the servant's towel of prayer firmly around ourselves, washing and drying the feet of those You so dearly love.

"Lord, we recognize that prayer is
powerful and effective,
active and strong,

16

efficient and able,

vigorous and forceful (Jas 5:16).

"Take the reins Lord and spur us into battle. With Your authority, we take the key of humility, unlocking the greatness of Your Kingdom into this world. With every battle won, every victory secured, may You be glorified and honored.

Amen."

> *"It isn't formulas or strategies, but the humility of prayer that allows the Spirit to use us in prayer."*
> *— Merodee*

***

> *"To enlist in God's victorious prayer army, humility must be sealed in our hearts and stamped across our minds. Prayer is in itself an act of humility, depending not on ourselves but in our loving Father and gracious Savior."*
> *— Meg*

***

> *"It was easy for me to have a practice of prayer based on answered prayers as opposed to the practice of prayer based on the character of God."*
> *— Allison*

***

17

Notes

1. Bill Johnson and Kris Vallotton, *The Supernatural Ways of Royalty: Discovering Your Rights and Privileges of Being a Son or Daughter of God* (Shippensburg: Destiny Image Publishers, 2006), 17.

2. Spiros Zodhiates Th.D., ed., *The Complete Word Study Dictionary: New Testament: For a Deeper Understanding of the Word*, rev. ed., (AMG International Inc., 1993), 1209-1210.

3. Elizabeth Pardi, Do You Know What 'Meek' of 'Meek and Humble of Heart' Really Means," Aleteia, March 22, 2017, https://aleteia.org/2017/03/22/do-you-know-what-meet-and-humble-of-heart-really-means/.

CHAPTER 2

A Sure Foundation
– The Rock of Faith

> *"Every day God answers. It isn't the big things but the little things that increase our faith."*
> *– Mark*

"When it is over, it's over!" His words struck hard against the fortress of prevailing faith. "Why don't you just give up and quit praying?"

Why didn't I quit? Why wouldn't I give up? Years of praying for this young couple's marriage hadn't produced any substantial results. The list of difficulties they faced scrolled endlessly, as if in bold print—a mocking denial of God's goodness and grace.

Yet, unceasing, contending prayer,
  intercessory prayer,
    warrior prayer,
      prophetic prayer,
        waiting prayer,
          surrendered prayer
formed a path deeper, wider than the onslaught of the enemy's attacks.

Later that day, I returned to my knees in prayer, again committing this young couple's marriage and small family to the authority of Jesus. She had prayed, fought, and eventually yielded to the inevitable reality of a marriage gone sour. In hopeless resignation, he had ventured down many ungodly paths, attempting to outrun God, himself, and their covenant relationship. Their small children were caught in the crosshairs—helpless victims of "friendly" fire.

"Lord, show me. I'll stop praying only when You tell me to stop. God, there are so many opinions and voices, but I need to know what You are saying about this situation." My pleas were racked with emotional intensity. "I have no intention to fight You on this. His friends applaud him, his family condones his choices, the church is silent, even his father agrees with the desolate condition of this marriage. But God . . . I can't . . . I won't quit praying for the restoration of their relationship until You give the word. But Lord, I need to know if I'm fighting against You. I will fight any enemy for as long as it takes, continuing to engage in the spiritual battle for this family, but I will not fight You."

How long I travailed in prayer, I'm not sure. The tears of intercession flowed freely as scriptural declaration ascended toward God's throne on their behalf. My whole body heaved with giant sobs—the struggle passionate, the physical and emotional toll of intercession undeniable.

Suddenly, an image pierced my consciousness. In the vision, I saw Jesus kneeling in a darkened, fog-filled garden, as the moon cast its timid glow over Him. Agonizing sobs that far surpassed my own wreathed His entire being. I realized immediately He was travailing in prayer for this same man and woman, their marriage and their family.

With my own prayers paling in comparison to His, I forgot about my intercession. I watched Him intently. Overwhelmed now by *His* sorrow, my heart only wanted to in some way comfort and bring Him peace. Quietly, I moved closer to Him, laying my hand upon His broad shoulder as it heaved with agonizing intensity. He would neither be comforted nor silenced before His Father as He pleaded for this little family—His broken, hurting children. The faint moonlight glistened off the tears pooling between His knees.

Slowly He rose to His feet, taking my hand in His. Together we ascended into the throne room of Heaven to our waiting Father. With an outstretched hand, He beckoned us—His Chosen Son and little daughter—to come and sit with Him. His great but gentle arms of comfort and strength circled us both as we sat upon His lap, weeping into His massive breast. Slowly, raw brokenness yielded to deep-rooted assurance and unshakeable confidence.

In stillness, we stayed where
    doubt has no place,
        love knows no bounds,
            hope fills every void,
                peace reaches perfection,
                    rest stills and calms,
                        and faith takes form.

As quickly as the vision began, it ended. From that moment on, I knew beyond all doubt that the answer was given; God had, indeed, spoken. I knew that with Jesus interceding for this marriage and family, victory was secure, the battle had been won.

I came away from the place of prayer with perfect peace and comfort knowing—sure beyond sure—it was finished. The devil and all his emissaries had lost. The price Jesus paid on the cross was enough to rebuild what everyone said was hopelessly broken. In the Presence of Jesus, nothing, absolutely nothing, is irreparable.

He spoke one directive to my heart, "Don't listen to his words, look into his eyes." Every time I encountered this young man, every time I heard the tears of his family, every time the words of hopelessness assaulted, I smiled and looked into their eyes, knowing that somewhere deep beyond feeling and fact was a truth far greater—God had poured His mercy and grace upon this marriage. He had made a way where there was no way.

A million decisions big and small paved the road to restoration. Dozens of people rose to stake themselves to this little family, walking them through to reconciliation and remarriage. Estranged husband and wife made a thousand painful, yet triumphant, steps of faith, giving their brave "Yes!" to God.

God gave the faith to pray and to keep on praying. He gave the solid word of promise on which faith could rest until the fulfillment followed.

> *"God is so big! If we speak His Word out, in faith we will see it come to pass." – Karli*

Personal Perspectives

God's promise gave Kate faith-filled assurance for her healing.

"Prayer is communicating with Almighty God, experiencing the Father's heart in and for people and situations, tasting His passion and compassion for souls.

"God allows every breath I take. Because I had respiratory issues most of my life, struggling to breathe, I have a literal understanding that God is the breath of life.

"Faith decrees and declares those things that are not as though they are (Rom 4:17). God's word does not return void but accomplishes His purposes (Is 55:11). When God gives us words to decree and declare, we know they will come to pass. No question! It's going to happen!

> *When He gives us the gift of faith, nothing can shake it.*

"Faith is substance; it's a sure thing, like holding something in your hand. You know you've got it and that it is so. You know that you can stand firm on the words that He is speaking either to you or for others. Nothing shakes that—nothing! You know that it is done and that you will see it physically manifest.

"At one point, when my health was bad, I was reading a book

written by a Christian author. The Holy Spirit made a sentence in the book come alive to me; through it, He gave me faith to believe for my healing. I knew I was going to see my deliverance from acute asthma attacks.

"That unshakable faith had nothing to do with me. It was a total gift from God for me to stand on, holding me firm in what He was saying. It did come to pass, but I had to wait for God's timing. I wanted it immediately, but that wasn't God's plan. Through the waiting, God taught me about His sovereignty and Lordship over my life.

"Medically, I was told I was heading for emphysema at a young age. By faith, I was able to say, 'No, I'm not.' I didn't have to work up the faith; God simply gave it to me. His voice was stronger than the diagnosis by medical professionals, declaring His will for me and becoming the rock I could stand on. It was a solid substance of truth and I knew it. I could respond, 'No that isn't going to happen to me because God says He is going to heal me. I'm not heading for emphysema.'

"That happened in 1990. After living with acute asthma attacks for many years, God did deliver me. God's goodness and kindness leads us to repentance and salvation (Rom 2:4).

"Faith is totally a work of Holy Spirit. **'Faith comes by hearing, and hearing by the word of God"** (Rom 10:17 NKJV). His truth builds faith, enabling us to believe in Him and what He says."

> *Anything in me that turns me toward God is of God.*
> *He is the Author and Originator of our faith.*
> *He will see it through to completion.*

Heather said,

"Prayer is not about me doing a specific thing I think should be done. God continually asks me to trust the Holy Spirit. I can beat myself up believing I didn't pray the right way or do the right things. I am re-thinking all of my so-called effectiveness I once took pride in, those things I worked hard to develop in prayer and felt right about.

"Prayer is a journey of trusting the moment—having faith in the silence and in the difficulties. During the struggles, I trust in the truth of who God is and the Word He has spoken."

"Our prayers may be awkward. Our attempts may be feeble. But since the power of prayer is in the One who hears it and not in the one who says it, our prayers do make a difference." [1]

Merodee shared about her crisis of faith.

"I had heard stories of the Holy Spirit falling so powerfully in Bible School that classes would be foregone to allow students to pray. I wanted that kind of experience too. When I went to Bible School, I felt disappointed and crushed, because it was not like that. But through a book report on Smith Wigglesworth, I saw the correlation between his meekness in prayer and the power of his ministry. Though I never asked anyone about it, I longed to see this meekness and power in action. I left Bible School feeling that moves of God were a then mark not a now mark. As a result, I stopped pursuing God.

"After that, I enrolled in nursing at university. While I was there, I experienced a crisis of my faith asking myself, 'Do I really believe in God?'

> *All of a sudden, I knew that if I gave my agreement to doubt, it would take over. I realized this would be a turning point in my faith.*

"It was such a strange place to be in. I thought, 'Mom and Dad believe and they aren't crazy. Pastor believes and he isn't crazy.'

"I joined Campus Crusade for Christ, expecting to attend faith-based Bible studies, but immediately we went out evangelizing. How could I evangelize when I was doubting my own relationship with the Lord?

"I remember approaching someone to share Jesus Christ with them. As I was going over the tract with them, something happened inside me. There was a flicker of hope: 'I do believe!' The more I shared my faith with others, the more my faith grew in me."

Christie also shared her experience.

"Recently my wrist was hurting so bad that I was wearing a brace and couldn't even hold my phone. A young man prayed for me, but it felt the same. Although he prayed again, it wasn't any better.

"I thought, 'Let's just skip it!'

"There are times when we don't think we need to pray, or don't think prayer will be effective. When we don't have faith ourselves, the faith of others can help us to stand our ground. The next day, it felt better, but I could feel some pain coming back. I said, 'No, this is over!'

"That happened about two months ago and my wrist is fine. The more we pray and see answers, the more we know the answers aren't coincidental. Prayer is effective; it works!

> *When you pray about the little things and see change, then it increases your faith for the bigger things.*

"Prayer is like a muscle you exercise. Like with anything else, you have to start small and build your way up. We need to keep utilizing prayer, exercising faith muscles until we pray without doubting.

"Often, we pray for something and do see God move, but immediately question, 'Did that really happen?' We need to be confident that God does answer and not second guess the results.

"Part of building faith is aligning ourselves to the truth. If we speak in the negative, it can become a stronghold because we've spoken it hundreds of times. Then when someone speaks a word of truth, we can't receive it because of the words of doubt we have continuously spoken.

"Faith isn't wishing, but rather putting the weight of prayer on what God says. Then we align our actions with what we believe and start moving in that direction."

Kari said,

"The other day I was praying for a woman who is an assistant pastor. She was going through a hard time and feeling deflated. She and her husband were both struggling. Every time I prayed for her, I heard, 'Arise! Arise!'

"I texted her, sharing what I was hearing. By faith, she was able to hold that word from Isaiah 60, **'Arise, shine, for your light has come, and the glory of the LORD rises upon you . . .'**

"I encouraged her that God wanted to be strong on her behalf. 'Let Him!' I said, 'Continue to speak that word.' As God confirmed His word to her, something internal started to blaze, allowing her to rise up by faith and move forward, believing God to be faithful. God had given me a word to awaken faith in someone else.

"In times like this, when I allow God to speak to me and share what He is saying, it increases my own faith. When the faith of others is activated and they become excited, it spurs me on to continue sharing what God is saying and doing. We can't afford to be timid, but need to go and share what He has spoken.

"I ask God to help me to have the faith I need to be a conduit. The Bible says that as I lay my hands on the sick, they will recover (Mk 16:17-18). In the past, I have laid hands on the sick and they weren't healed. I became discouraged and afraid, thinking, 'What if I pray again and no one is healed?'

"I had to stop thinking like that, but rather to renew my mind according to what the Bible teaches. Because God doesn't complicate things, we have to keep prayer simple too, 'Be well! You are healed!'

"Every situation is different. It's key to hear what God is saying in each situation and to remember that there are no formulas for prayer. God wants us to come into a personal relationship with Him, not be focused on finding a formula.

"I've shrunk back a bit when my faith gets rocked or when I haven't heard well. But the Bible says that ' . . . **though the righteous fall seven times, they rise again'** (Prv 24:16).

"God always picks me up and gives me another opportunity. When He does, I take it!"

Lois adds,

"Faith and prayer increase exponentially as you continue to practice them. Whether you are learning to ride a bike, swim or something else, you have to practice without expecting everything to instantly work out. Faith is the same. When we step out and push the boundaries to see what the Lord will do, completely relying on Him, faith builds.

> *Pray and expect! We are supposed to ask big because we have a big God.*

"As we see God move, our faith grows; the more He moves the more our faith increases. Prayer and faith go together like a hand in a glove. You can't have one without the other. To build faith, continually press into the Lord through prayer, meditation, listening and seeing Him work."

God gave Dennis an illustration of faith through a vision.

"I was meditating on the Lord one day and had a vision of a large field with huge equipment of various kinds. In the vision, the Lord asked, 'Where are you in this picture?'

"I said, 'God, I have no idea.'

"God told me I was the draw pin which connects the tractor

to the equipment. He showed me that the tractor is the Word of God, the fuel in the tractor is Holy Spirit and the driver is the will of the Father. The implements are the gifts and operations of Holy Spirit.

"God needs someone who is reading the Word, moving in the Spirit and going with the will of the Father. He can use any one of us when we are doing these things.

"No one cares about the draw pin except a farmer. A smaller piece called the cotter pin prevents the draw pin from bouncing out of the hitch. This little pin fills the place of our inadequacy; it is called faith. Faith keeps us in the Word no matter what has happened. It keeps us in the Spirit and the will of the Father even when the going gets tough. When you are positioned with faith where God wants you, He is able to use you."

Karin says,

"A lot of my prayer takes place in my bedroom talking to God and Him speaking to me. There is a certainty that it is Him. To some degree, people can comfort you, but when you hear from the Lord it's as good as done. Nobody can take away what He has said.

"When you have spent time in Scripture and with the Lord in prayer, you go from grace to grace and faith to faith. Charles Spurgeon said that prayer and faith are so tightly interconnected that if you convince someone that prayer is of no use, they will soon lose their faith. That is why the enemy targets our faith and prayer.

"When someone starts to pray, they are not far from God. He is drawing them to Himself and they will have an enriched walk with Him."

God gave Amanda^C His word as an anchor for her faith to hold on to during an important time in her life.

> "Before Christmas, my grandfather received the news that he had stage four cancer in his prostate. When I asked God what the truth was in this situation, I felt Him tell me that He was going to be glorified in it. I knew that cancer would go from stage four to stage three to stage two until it was all gone.

> "When the doctors performed various tests and found a darkened area on his hip, they wanted to do a biopsy. Although I was initially upset about the diagnosis, after God gave me His word of promise, I could begin to thank Him. I started praying in tongues,[2] getting louder and louder until I was shouting and praising God. I don't think I had ever prayed like that before.

> "God has been healing him and shrinking cancer in his body. Based on what they can see now, they believe the area used to have cancer, but the bone has grown back into its place properly."

Unlocking the Legacy

**"Now faith is the substance of things hoped for,
the evidence of things not seen."
Hebrews 11:1 (NKJV)**

Faith is having complete trust or confidence in someone or something. As Christians, we place our trust and confidence in God. Our faith rests on the sure foundation of God's character, power and goodness, and faithfulness to His promise. Faith is undaunted by circumstance or natural ability; faith rests on the foundational truth of the Bible.

Kathryn Kuhlman said, "at the heart of your faith is a Person, the very Son of the living God, whose power is greater than any enemy you face."[3] He is the standard—the unchangeable plumb line of certainty.

Hope resides in the *mind* and looks to the future for help. The voice of hope declares, "Someday God will heal me. Later, it will happen. Sometime, God will show me." Hope has an assurance that God is and that He can, but hope falls short of knowing that God is available right now, today.

"Now faith is!" Faith dwells within the *heart* and exists now, right here amid our circumstances. Faith is a tangible substance, solid and sure. It is the evidence of what we don't yet see with our natural eyes but know as an eternal reality.

Faith takes back territory from doubt and unbelief,
    looks in the face of Goliath and tells him to fall,
        surpasses human ability, holding firmly to God,
            stands unquestionable against reason and
                laughs in the face of the enemy.

When an angel came to a young girl named Mary with an impossible promise, he said,

"For no word from God will ever fail."
Luke 1:37

Though the angel's words made no sense, the word of God superseded natural circumstance creating evidence and substance—a child born of a virgin. This verse more accurately stated reads, "with God's word comes the power to fulfill it." When God speaks, it's done!

"The currency of Heaven is faith." – Mark

Prayer is the spiritual compass that directs us ever Godward. No matter the direction life may steer us, faith continually points our seeking heart to God. By faith, we find God's sovereign hand in every situation, regardless of His timing or how He moves.

"Prayer is conscious of the need, while faith supplies it.

Prayer never obtains anything from God unless faith is present. Faith never receives anything from God unless prayer makes the petition . . . Prayer is the voice of the soul, while faith is the hand." [4]

Paul said, **"The righteous will live by faith"** (Rom 1:17). We have within the Gospel a righteousness that propels us from faith to ever-increasing faith,

    taking hold of courage, accelerating in power,
        sharpening in focus, surging forward with force,
            tenacious in vigor and
                audacious in proclamation.

Christy reminded us that praying about little things builds faith for praying through bigger things. There are many times we struggle to apply foundational truth in prayer, needing more faith to believe God's word over circumstantial facts. Faith and fact consistently collide.

The fact *was* the walls of Jericho were impermeable;
    the truth *is* they fell with a shout.

      The fact *was* the Red Sea was impassable;
          the truth *is* the wind of God parted the way.

      The fact *was* the enemies of Israel were strong;
    the truth *is* God is stronger.

Facts change as quickly as the weather on the prairies, but truth remains eternally constant.

Often, it's with reluctance that I place my wavering hand into God's mighty one. It takes faith to surrender to God, trusting and resting in Him. God responds to even our faintest faith, but **"without faith it is impossible to please God"** (Heb 11:6). He has already given to each of us **"a measure of faith"** (Rom 12:3 NKJV). Faith isn't something we work up in ourselves, but rather a gift of grace.

"We look away from the natural realm and we fasten our gaze onto Jesus who *birthed faith* within us and who leads us forward into *faith's perfection*. His example is this: Because his heart was focused on the joy of knowing that you would be his, he endured the agony of the cross and conquered its

**humiliation, and now sits exalted at the right
hand of the throne of God!"
Hebrews 12:2 TPT
(Emphasis mine)**

Faith begins with God and He brings it to maturity. Faith is birthed and perfected in and by Him. We will only realize the full potential of the legacy God has for us as we pray and live by faith.

Jesus talked about varying levels of faith which still exist today. John said of the spiritual elite, **". . . they still would not believe in him . . . For this reason they could not believe"** (Jn 12:37-39). Yet a Roman officer was able to access the reservoir of **"great faith"** (Mt 8:10).

"The life of faith is built around promises given, tests encountered and fulfillment enjoyed. For every promise, there is a test, and with every test there is grace, mercy and the strength of the Almighty to see us through." [5]

Jesus encouraged His followers,

**". . . Truly I tell you, if you have faith as small as a mustard seed, you can say to this mountain, 'Move from here to there,' and it will move. Nothing will be impossible for you."
Matthew 17:20**

Faith is the channel through which prayer flows unpolluted and unhindered. Every legacy unlocked and every spiritual victory won comes by faith.

There's hope! Prayer infused with even the smallest amount of faith has the power to move Heaven and earth on our behalf. It is neither the size of our prayer nor the size of our faith but the size of our God that determines the outcome. God calls for prayer, not panic, to be our first response to adversity. When we most feel like fainting, faith takes hold, supernaturally releasing the flow of Heaven around us.

"Once God has revealed that something is absolutely true, no further question remains. It's as if a veil is ripped from your eyes, and having seen the truth, nothing can make you go back." [6]

Such is the confidence and assurance of knowing God's will for a situation. We unlock the legacy God has for us by laying hold of faith in prayer. The impossible becomes possible as God works in and through faith-filled prayer.

Taking Territory

"Lord, **'Increase our faith'** (Lk 17:5)! Because **'faith comes from hearing and hearing from the word of God,'** we open wide our hearts and minds to receive Your word and hold it as irreplaceably precious (Rom 10:17 NKJV). We come to You in prayer with the **'sword of the Spirit, which is the word of God'** (Eph 6:17). Open our ears to be receptive to the *"now"* words You are speaking. May we not be satisfied with hope for tomorrow, while faith stands and knocks at the door today. Seal your *"now"* words with power upon our hearts, giving us boldness to proclaim them with authority into the world.

" **'Your word is a lamp for (our) feet, and a light on (our) path,'** guiding us in prayer to bring Your Light to those held in dark prisons within the enemy camp (Ps 119:105). We take the key of faith, secure and steadfast, unlocking Your word over those bound by lies and deception. Through faith, we proclaim, "Now is Your word accomplished. Now is your word fulfilled."

"With faith, we declare that God **'exists and that he rewards those who earnestly seek him'** (Heb 11:6). By faith we consider You faithful to all You have promised. By faith, we bless those around us, including our enemies. It is by faith that we **'choose to be mistreated along with the people of God rather than to enjoy the fleeting pleasures of sin,'** yet persevere because we see You, the invisible One (Heb 11:6-27).

"With those who have gone before us, we turn the key of faith conquering kingdoms and administering justice,

gaining what has been promised to us,

shutting the mouths of lions,

quenching the fury of the flames

of the evil one,
escaping the edge of sharpened swords,
turning weakness into strength,
becoming powerful in battle,
routing enemy armies, and
bringing the dead back to life.

"Such is the destiny of those who lay hold of the key of faith that You have placed in our hands (Heb 11:33-35).

"Yet, we presume nothing, for there have been many faith-filled followers of Jesus who were
tortured for their faith,
faced jeers and flogging,
put in chains and imprisoned,
stoned or killed by the sword.
They barely had enough to wear,
were destitute and mistreated,
wandered in deserts and mountains,
lived in caves or holes in the ground,
were commended for their faith, and
didn't receive what was promised.

"Oh, how powerful is the key of faith that You have placed in our hands! It's a faith to endure in the waiting and testing (Heb 11:35-40). We trust You with the timing and the manner in which You respond to all our prayers.

"We are confident and bold in faith, turning this precious key with steel-faced tenacity, knowing that the Author, and Perfecter, guides our hands and orders our steps. With faith, we look into the face of the enemy and say, "Back off! God has spoken! He has declared our victory and we are pressing into the promised inheritance He has for us and our household, our city and nation."

"Today, right now, we take the legacy God has entrusted to us by faith. **'We do not belong to those who shrink back and are destroyed, but to those who have faith and are saved'** (Heb 10:39).

"Thank You, Lord, for this key of mountain moving, lion taming, devil defeating faith.

Amen."

> *"Faith is a total work of Holy Spirit. Faith comes by hearing and hearing by the Word of God.' "* — Kate

***

> *"To pray and see that God is answering prayer is essential to our faith. If you are losing faith, surround yourself with people of faith. Faith will lift you up."* — Karin

***

> *"I asked, 'But God, what if I pray and nothing happens?' He said, 'It's none of your business! Your job is to pray.' "* — Betty

***

Notes

1. Max Lucado, Goodreads, https://www.goodreads.com/quotes/813471-our-prayers-may-be-awkward-our-attempts-may-be-feelbe.

2. Dennis & Rita Bennett, *The Holy Spirit & You: A Guide to the Spirit-Filled Life* (Newberry, Bridge-Logos Publishers, 1971, 1998, 56.
(Dennis & Rita Bennett explain praying in tongues as, "Speaking in tongues is prayer with and in the Spirit — it is our spirit speaking to God, inspired by the Holy Spirit.")

3. Kathryn Kuhlman, *I Believe in Miracles: Streams of Healing from the Heart of a Woman of Faith*, rev.upd., (Gainesville, Bridge-Logos Publishers, 2001), 194.

4. Kuhlman, *I Believe in Miracles*, 87-88.

5. Frank Damazio, *From Barrenness to Fruitfulness: Restoration for the Heart and Soul of Leaders* (Ventura, Regal Books, 1998), 65.

6. Chuck D. Pierce and Rebecca Wagner Sytsema, *Possessing Your Inheritance: Moving Forward in God's Covenant Plan for Your Life* (Ventura, Renew, 1990), 128.

CHAPTER 3

Pick Up the Sword – A Mighty Weapon

> *"Take the Word, speak the Word and pray the Word. When you do this and keep doing it, you will see the changes happen."*
> *– Candice*

As soon as the door closed behind him, I ran to the bedroom collapsing on my knees beside the bed. "Lord, change him! Please! God, I don't know what to do; I'm done; I've got nothing left to give."

My prayer was an all too familiar plea oozing out from not just a broken marriage but a broken life. Tension filled every moment we spent together. Psychological abuse scarred my mind and bruised my soul, leaving indelible marks too deep for human eyes. It was a cycle that began days into our marriage and continued unabated—a cycle of mutual destruction that we both tried and failed to change.

As I wept, I heard the Lord speak sharply—not in my ears, but into my heart in a way that stunned me, "Leave him to me. It's *you* who *needs* to change."

God's words were not condemning but, nonetheless, assertive and unwavering. Even though the abuse was identifiable and the games of emotional volleyball real, I knew, beyond a doubt, God was right. He saw what I was obviously blind to.

Rather than prayer, my petitions flowed from a cesspool of self-loathing. God had heard enough of my bitter grumbling filled with self-pity. God was bringing change, but not how I wanted nor with whom I had hoped. At that moment, God presented me with two options: living pitifully or powerfully. The choice was mine.

Intense brokenness thrust me into God's loving arms and brokenness kept me there. A new level of surrender was necessary for Him to do in me what must be done. I needed radical spiritual surgery removing every self-defacing system I had previously relied on

self-protection and self-righteousness,
selfish desires and selfish ambitions,
self-reliance and self-conceit,
self-service and self-gratification.

Each me-centered motivation was a cancerous tumor of sin, destroying everyone around me. Such invasive intervention from God would go beyond a single moment, day or week, but rather a necessary continuum throughout my life. Every rotten attitude and fermenting mindset had to go. I had to fully acknowledge that I was filled with dis-ease, contaminating my relationships with an infectious malady.

My tone changed to deep and submissive resolve, "Whatever it takes, Lord, change me."

Shortly afterward, I was watching a Christian television program called *100 Huntley Street*. One of the guests talked about declaring the word of God over personal circumstances and relationships. My spirit grabbed hold of the concept, knowing it was a strategic prayer tool that I desperately needed.

Almost immediately I began to pick up the word of God in a new way, learning to use it as a mighty weapon in my daily struggles. God gave me many passages to declare and decree in prayer over myself and the things I was facing.

Through Psalm 84, I began to proclaim God's promise to take me through all difficulties. I prayed with a new confidence knowing that God was with me. I knew I was secure in Him.

> "My soul yearns, even faints for you Lord. The
> place I want most to be is near You, near Your
> altar of sacrifice. You are my King and my God
> and I will continually praise You. I am blessed!
> My strength is in You. I have set my whole heart
> on pursuing Your face and Your Kingdom. I know
> that there are difficult places that You are taking
> me *through*. Yes, Lord! You are leading me *through*!
> You are not abandoning me in this valley, but You
> are leading me *through*! Even when I pass *through*
> the places of weeping, I am digging wells that will
> sustain and strengthen others who also walk this
> path. I ask for deep pools of refreshing for every-
> one else who will journey this valley. I am not weak,
> fragile or broken. You are taking me from strength
> to strength . . . my whole trust is in You, Lord.
> My past does not dictate my future.
> Today is a new day."
> (My adapted prayer version)

I also began to declare Psalm 1:1-3 and other Bible verses over
my husband. By inserting his name, I personalized these Scriptures in
prayer declaration, annihilating my negative mindsets and the devil's
lies with God's mighty sword.

> "My husband is blessed! Lord, he does not walk
> in step with the wicked. Nor does he stand in the
> way that sinners take. He doesn't waste his time
> sitting in the company of mockers. My husband
> delights in the law of the Lord. Oh God, he takes
> great delight in Your word, meditating on it day
> and night. While he is working or resting bring
> Your Word into his thoughts and settle it deep in
> his heart. My husband is like a tree planted by
> streams of water. Oh Lord, cause his spiritual
> roots to go down deep, drawing strength from
> You. You are his Source of all good things. My
> husband's life will yield fruit in every season,

> **continually being productive. Lord, You know the
> season he is in now and the one You are drawing
> him into in the future. You have determined that
> my husband's life will not wither. Your portion for
> him is not barrenness, brokenness or waste, but
> whatever he does will prosper. God, You are watch-
> ing over him and making all his ways straight as
> You lead him into righteousness. He will
> be an example to many men, young and old, show-
> ing the difference You make in our lives."**
> **(My adapted prayer version)**

Rather than dramatic or instantaneous changes in either my own or my husband's behavior, God worked out a consistent and continuous process of transformation in us both.

What's more, the sword of the Spirit exposed my perverse attitudes and behaviors, allowing God to increasingly deal with my internal garbage. Many of the problems in our marriage were directly connected to the invasive, ungodly roots in me. (Shocking but true!)

There were other verses I began to declare over our marriage and our family:

repenting through Psalm 51,
seeking protection through Psalm 91,
gaining comfort through Psalm 23,
praise and worship through Psalm 149,
proclaiming victory through Psalm 30,
and declaring wisdom, understanding and insight
through Psalm 119:97-104.

The word of God became a mighty prayer weapon of warfare. With time and practice, I became increasingly skilled in its use. God knew that the greatest motivation for me to learn how to utilize this new key of unlocking legacy was through applying it in prayer for those I loved the most. The more I allowed God's word to penetrate and change me, the more I saw changes in others.

We often want instant and miraculous; God works through the process. The sword-wielding process, once learned, can be applied strategically to every area of life.

Years later, I look at my husband with awe, wondering, "Who are you? Where did you come from? How did such dramatic transformation occur?" Out of the ashes of the old, God has recreated a new and amazing man worthy of honor and respect. The husband, father and man he once was is only a faint memory. By God's marvelous grace, he truly has become a Psalms 1 man of righteousness, loving God deeply, while prospering at everything he does.

The changes in my own life, although no less drastic, continue—some slowly, others quickly. Perhaps the greatest change is in the way I pray. God taught me how to use the Bible, His powerful key to unlocking the legacy of transformational change. We accomplish this by speaking God's Word back to Him, activating His authority over circumstances and into the lives of those around us.

Personal Perspectives

Kari says that the greatest miracle she has experienced is in the life of her son.

"For a long time after I accepted Christ, I had a desire to write the Word of God. Often, I would be writing the Word and wondering, 'Is this making a difference?' There is something powerful about writing out the Word, seeing it and then speaking it out as it downloads into your heart. You can know the Bible, but suddenly it takes root in your heart; from the root of truth comes faith to believe; then through believing, prayer takes form and everything changes.

"The Holy Spirit increases our thirst and hunger for more, causing us to feed on the Word and grow in faith. When we speak the Word of God, knowing He is faithful, His Word gains power in our lives, bringing changes in the atmosphere. It is essential to acquire a revelation knowledge of the Word of God, speaking it out and calling those things that are not as if they were (Rom 4:17).

41

"I was the first one in our family to come into a relationship with Jesus Christ twenty-seven years ago. Shortly after, I was in the shower washing my hair and simply said, 'Okay God, I pray for my mom's salvation.' Because I didn't have much faith, I thought, 'Yeah, right!' Within a year, however, my mom accepted Jesus Christ. God is so incredibly good that He still answers prayer even when faith is small.

"When we pray, obeying the Holy Spirit's leading, God is faithful and answers. Prayer comes from knowing the Word of God and responding to the Holy Spirit within us. The same power that raised Jesus from the dead is living inside of us (Rom 8:11). God in us! That's huge! We can tap into His power.

> *We speak out the Word because the law of kindness is always on our tongue.*[1]

"My son was three months old when I gave my life to Jesus. Ever since, I have prayed over him, declaring and decreeing the attributes for people in ministry. **'(You) are above reproach. (You) are the husband of one wife. (You) are temperate, self-controlled, hospitable, able to teach, not given to drunkenness, not violent but gentle, not quarrelsome and not a lover of money. (You) manage your family well, making sure your children obey you with proper respect'** (Ti 1:6-9).

"It's not that he is perfect, but he's twenty-four years old now and isn't going to bars, drinking or doing drugs. He's everything I prayed from the Word.

"We have such a short window of time with our children; suddenly, those childhood years are gone. The fruit I am seeing in my son illustrates the power of God's Word. Yes, I prayed for him, but the real power is in the Word of God not my prayers. Sometimes it seems to take so long to see the results of prayer, but if we just keep praying the Word, we *will* see it come to pass.

"After my divorce, I was heartbroken and cried out to the Lord, 'I can't do this. How can I be a good mother to my son?'

"When my son was still very young, my pastor said to me, 'Don't ever think that your son lacks any good thing (Ps 34:10). Having a father in the house doesn't mean he is a great father to his kids. Don't let anyone talk down about your son lacking anything because he doesn't have a father. God is a father to the fatherless and a husband to the widow' (Ps 68:5-6).

"I spoke that truth emphatically over my son, 'Montana, you lack no good thing. God is a Father to the fatherless and a Husband to the widow. We are good!' He has never felt sorry for himself. He knows that he can go to God for wisdom, help and guidance.

"Recently I cleaned out his room and found his old journal. I forgot how as a child he would sit on the floor, often with his dog beside him, writing the Word of God in a journal. His journal is filled with Scriptures from Proverbs and Psalms. It's a treasure. When he was little and saw me writing out the Word of God, he did the same.

"God has planted that Word into his heart and made it grow. I take no credit for it. I have to say that my son's life is the greatest miracle I have witnessed.

"I always took him to church when he was little. While I was in the service, He received ministry in Children's Church. I determined to raise him in a healthy environment without fighting and tension. Even though there was a lot of friction between us, I was taught from early not to put his father down. Montana loves the Lord and shows respect and honor for both me and his dad. That's a miracle.

"As hard as being a single mother was, I wouldn't trade it for anything. No matter how tough life got, God proved Himself faithful in every circumstance. All along the way, I saw God's favor. When you put God first, He takes care of everything else (Mt 6:33).

"Declaring God's Word filters through every area of life. When I walk, I speak the Word of God over my community and the people around me. Declaring and decreeing biblical truth by repeating the words God has already spoken back to Him is powerful!

"I've always had painful cold sores that would crack and bleed. I believed the doctors when they told me it's because some people are born with the virus. Recently, when another cold sore appeared, I decided to take authority over cold sores, just like Jesus did with the fig tree (Mk 11:12-14, 20-25). 'I curse you cold sore at the root. You shrivel up and die.' It was there a little, but it didn't get any bigger.

"The Bible says, **'the kingdom of Heaven suffers violence, and the violent take it by force'** (Mt 11:12 NKJV). I said, 'You darn devil. I am speaking the Word over my situation. You are not going to win this.' It may seem odd because it was only a cold sore, but it was time to say, 'Enough!'

"Sometimes God asks us, 'How badly do you want this?' We have to be tenacious to gain the victory over situations.

" **'The redeemed of the LORD say so'** (Ps 107:2). 'So devil, you get your hands off of me. I am redeemed and I say so. My inheritance is health and healing not all sorts of other things.'

"A while ago, I started having hot flashes because I'm going through a change in life. I thought, 'Hold it! I don't need to deal with this.' After a couple of months of taking authority over it, I rarely have a hot flash. Because the Word of God is powerful, we don't have to accept whatever the devil throws our way. We have to match our words with what God says rather than agreeing with the people around us or our situation.

> *God is listening. The angels are listening.*
> *The Host of Heaven is waiting for a command.*
> *God wants us to speak His Word with expectation.*

"God needs our voices; He needs us to speak. It is one thing to read the Bible, but God tells us to open our mouths declaring His Word and His works. When we do, we will see things change."

Barb shares how the Word of God became powerful in her life.

"I was told to pray for small healings to build my faith. I sat in my easy chair, closed my eyes and asked the Lord what He wanted me to do now that I was saved and baptized in the Holy Spirit. Suddenly, ticker-tape flashed before my closed eyes, and on it was written Mark 3:15.

"I didn't know what Mark 3:15 said, but after three or four flashes, I thought I better look it up. I read, '. . . **to have power to heal sicknesses, and to cast out devils.**'

"I asked God, 'Where?'

"He said, 'The back forty.' I knew God was telling me to minister to those right close by.

"My journey in healing and deliverance ministry began with the Word of God like ticker-tape running before my eyes. When I pray for someone, I often pray the Word. The Bible shouldn't be something we just read. It's personal and it's powerful!

"My husband and I have seen many healings and miracles (spiritually and physically): Belles Palsy, rheumatism, varicose veins, and migraine headaches. I had an underactive thyroid, but we prayed and it became completely normal. That was over forty years ago, but every time a physician checks me, it's still normal. Once, I even ran my hand over our dog's back and asked the Lord to take all arthritic pain away. Later he was running and jumping around so happy.

"We learned the truth of Matthew 16:19, **'I will give you the keys of the kingdom of Heaven; whatever you bind on earth will be bound in Heaven, and whatever you loose on earth will be loosed in Heaven.'** Early in our prayer journey, we learned to take the Word of God and release it through prayer."

Sharon was initiated into using the Sword of the Spirit, God's Word, in prayer by divine initiation.

"I have never been to Bible School and haven't even read the whole Bible. Praying Scripture is something God has put in me.

"When I read the Bible or God gives me a portion of Scripture, I take it personally. Like Isaiah 59:21, ' **"As for me, this is my covenant with them," says the LORD, "My Spirit, who is on you, will not depart from you, and my words that I have put in your mouth will always be on your lips, on the lips of your children and on the lips of their descendants — from this time on and forever," says the LORD.'**

"I declare and decree Scripture for myself and my children. God has given me His Word to lay hold of, praying it personally.

"When I was first saved, I was hungry for the Word of God and studied it a lot. However, I don't memorize the Word so I can pray it. Rather, it is something that flows naturally. I honestly can't take credit for it. I often struggle to read the

Bible, at times wondering afterward what I just read. Yet, when I pray, the Word is constantly on my tongue.

"The Word of God is a weapon of warfare that He equips us with. God puts within us the Sword of His Spirit to use as He wills.

"When God speaks to me, it will usually be from the Word. It's like having a photographic memory, only without having read the whole Bible. There is great boldness in praying the Word of God and personally declaring it. God humbles us in the process."

Charlene talked about the corporate aspect of declaring God's Word in prayer.

"One Sunday, we knew that we could either have church or we could pray. We chose to pray, worship and talk about how God's Word doesn't return void (Is 55:10-11). God desires that we use His Word to pray.

"I said, 'We're going to worship and then as we are in the Presence of God before His throne, we're going to petition Him, praying the Word.'

"We began praying Scripture as a group in complete unity. We prayed about the parable of the seed (Lk 8:4-15). We prayed that everything the Holy Spirit was doing would be protected and covered. Then we prayed the seed for all those involved wouldn't be stolen or choked out by the weedy things of the world. We prayed the seed that Holy Spirit already planted would grow deep and bear fruit. Then we prayed the Ephesians prayer for knowing the love of God, revelation, knowledge and wisdom (Eph 1:16-19).

"The situation we were praying for grew worse before things changed for the better. At one point, I said, 'Lord, I'm not looking at this with natural eyes.' We kept praying the Word of God with nothing to lose. Things needed to change, but we had to keep going to God, through prayer, speaking His truth.

> *Nothing was ethereal. It was all very real.*
> *You could tell when God answered or when He didn't.*
> *That's scary, but it's the only way to pray.*

"The whole time, we needed to listen to the Holy Spirit. We often felt like we were on a roller coaster, but everything shifted."

Kate also learned about praying Scripture in a corporate setting.

"The people in the prayer group would speak about the Bible, repeat the Word of God and in faith rely on it by praying it back to God in declaration. When I heard the Word of God prayed like that my ears were open for more.

"Prayer is
    decreeing and declaring the Word of God
        worshipping, thanking and praising the Lord,
            speaking God's Word into specific
                situations and people's lives,
then standing upon the Word until we see change.

"In it all, we enjoy the Lord's Presence, casting our crowns at His feet. Anything that is of God in my life, originates from Him. It has nothing to do with me. God alone gets all the thanksgiving, praise and glory for anything godly that comes from my life.

"In humility, there is a continuation of the awe of the Lord and His sovereignty over our lives, as well as a deepening in our reverence for Him.

"Scripture talks about praying without ceasing, referring to living a life of prayer (1 Thes 5:16-18). We can be in an attitude of prayer no matter where we are or what we are doing. I want to always be aware of the Spirit's Presence, listening to His voice and feeling the Father's heart for a situation. Prayer is more than a lifestyle, it *is* my life.

"When you realize prayer is so multifaceted, it's exciting. We cannot limit God by putting Him in a box. There is always a new way to learn to pray and a new way of walking with the Holy Spirit in prayer. Declaring and decreeing His Word is His ministry working through us."

Emily keeps prayer simple.

"Scripture in prayer is my sword. If the Lord doesn't give me a specific Scripture, I will search for one, praying that portion. Prayer is never despair or depression. Sometimes there is weeping but never discouragement. Prayer comes from the place of restoration and victory as I read Scripture out loud to the Lord and declare it over people or circumstances.

"I pick a Scripture that means something to me about the situation and I stay on it. Even when I don't see answers, I keep praying until the Lord reveals His truth. For more intense things, I pray to Him through Scripture, but I don't dwell on it. Too often, we make prayer complicated, but I try to keep it simple.

"God has told me to keep my heart clean. If I'm going to be used by God, I must have a clean heart. My heart is a filter; a clean heart allows Him to flow through it without resistance."

Audrey prays the Word of God in a slightly different way.

"When my life wasn't in a good place, God brought me through a process of discovering who and what I believed Him to be.

"There was a book on a table at a friend's house. Even though I didn't like reading, I grabbed the book and asked if I could read it. When I started reading it, I couldn't put it down, highlighting and underlining portions from cover to cover. God used that book to allow me to discover for myself who He is.

"After I read numerous other books and connected with television evangelists, I decided I needed to read the Bible. I haven't stopped; I want more and more. God shows us so much through His Word. It was through reading the Bible that I was drawn to attend a Spirit-filled church.

"Communication with God through prayer became more conversational. I discovered there's more to prayer than reciting something and hoping for the best. As my faith grew, I took Scriptures, rewriting them word for word, and inserting my name into the text to make them personal. **I am a child of the Most High God'** (Gal 3:26-29).

"The more I did it the more I saw the results of praying this way. I felt empowered when I prayed His Word through rewriting Scripture. When I'm heavy-hearted, by getting into Scripture, rewriting and making it personal in prayer, I come away feeling totally victorious. God demonstrates over and over how I can trust Him and His Word.

"It's so much more effective when we write prayer than when we just think or say it. Somehow, we process it more getting it into our hearts."

Unlocking the Legacy

"For the word of God is alive and active. Sharper than any double-edged sword, it penetrates even to dividing soul and spirit, joints and marrow; it judges the thoughts and attitudes of the heart."
Hebrews 4:12

God brought Ezekiel to the middle of a valley full of dry bones (Ez 37). Rather than a quick peek, God deliberately led Ezekiel back and forth through the desolate and barren valley until the desperateness of the situation gripped his heart. **"I saw a great many bones on the floor of the valley, bones that were very dry."**

Then God asked Ezekiel, **"Can these bones live?"**

Wisely, Ezekiel responded, **"You alone know."**

Then God spoke a life-giving word over the bones. Nothing happened—nothing! Immediately, God instructed Ezekiel to speak those same words He had just spoken without any result. Don't expect anything rational about this God encounter. If God speaks and nothing is changed, how dare any one of us presume to speak those words with a different result?

By faith, however, Ezekiel spoke the Word of the Lord. Bones instantly clattered and clanked into motion, coming together in perfect formation, tendons and flesh appeared and perfect skin covered each restored body. Sun-bleached, dry bones took lifeless human form as a man of faith spoke the Word of God.

Again, God spoke; again, nothing happened. Again, Ezekiel repeated God's words commanding breath to enter the dead bodies and **"they came to life and stood up on their feet — a vast army."**

It intrigues me that God's voice wasn't enough. I honestly don't understand why He needed someone, anyone, to agree with Him, speaking His Word with authority. The rehearsing, restating, re-establishing of God's Word continues to have a supernatural effect wherever it is declared.

The nation of Israel at that time was spiritually dry, desperately hopeless and cut off from God. The bones coming back to life and forming a powerful army became a living illustration, declaring both to Ezekiel and to us that nothing is impossible with God (Lk 1:37).

How similar are many of our current nations today? God is looking for faith-filled people who will believe the Word and speak life into dry places, bringing

hope into hopeless situations,

restoration into broken and

dismembered relationships, and

faith to the unfaithful or faithless.

We cannot afford to forget how powerful the Holy Spirit within us is. As He directs us to speak again His living Word, it becomes a lightning sword infusing death with life.

> **"Take the helmet of salvation and**
> **the sword of the Spirit,**
> **which is the word of God."**
> **Ephesians 6:17**

God has given us His Word, but it waits for believing hearts to speak it out by faith. As we declare and decree God's Word over people, places and situations, the victory Christ already won at the cross is powerfully released.

> *"The Bible is a written Word of God and because it*
> *is written it is confined and limited by the necessities of*
> *ink and paper and leather. The voice of God, however,*
> *is alive and free as the sovereign God is free. 'The words*
> *that I speak unto you, they are spirit, and they are life'*
> *(Jn 6:63). The life is in speaking the words . . . It is*
> *the present Voice that makes the written Word all-pow-*
> *erful. Otherwise, it would lie locked in slumber within*
> *the covers of a book."* [2]

There is an army waiting to rise out of the desert valleys of desolation and defeat,

discouragement and disbelief,

devastation and despair,

deception and disillusionment

discontent and discord.

Who will speak, activating authority, declaring life and restoration, striking the mark in the spirit realm? In so doing, we reclaim for this generation the promises and purposes of God. He, more than anyone, is anxious to see His church rise to their feet, strong and ready to engage in Kingdom work. He has given us the key of His Word to unlock the legacy.

Taking Territory

"Oh Lord, how we love Your Word! We meditate on it all day long. Your living Word is with us, making us wiser than our enemies. We have more insight than all our teachers and more understanding than our elders, because of the truth and wisdom that comes from Your Word. Thank You, that moment by moment and day by day You continue to lead and teach us through Your Word (Ps 119:97-104).

"You send Your Word and heal us (Ps 107:20). All things are held together by the Word of Your mouth (Col 1:17).

"We choose to come into agreement with the Word of truth,
    declaring with our mouths and
        believing in our hearts that what You say will
            be established and do all You sent it to do.
    Your Word will never return void
  but will soften hardened hearts,
        causing life to rise from dead places
          producing all You desire.
             Joy and gladness will go before us,
        Our lives will be fruitful and productive
    for Your glory and renown
      (Is 55:10-13).

"We speak Your truth into situations and over lives, changing atmospheres from darkness to light over entire regions. We declare Your Heavenly Host active, like flames of fire, over our families and communities (Heb 1:7). Your desire for us is not for evil but for good.

Your plans are to prosper us and not to harm us, bringing hope and releasing expectations for the future. As we pray, You are listening and making Yourself known to us in new and surprising ways (Jer 29:11-13).

"The enemy will not have his way. We declare that we are strong in the Lord and in His mighty power. Today, we put on the full armor of God, taking our stand against the devil's schemes. We refuse to struggle against flesh and blood as we take our stand against rulers, authorities and powers of this dark world, and the spiritual forces of evil. Teach us how to effectively wield the Sword of the Spirit, the Word of God. We are mighty in You, alert in prayer (Eph 6:10-18).

"No weapon formed against us will prosper, for You are with us (Is 54:17). We choose to hide Your Word in our hearts, preserving it in our memory (Ps 119:11). Give us Your wisdom to know what to speak in every situation (Lk 12:12). May our words be in perfect agreement with Yours. You have not called us to silence but to declare Your Word time and time again before Your throne.

"Give us greater boldness, Lord, to speak Your declarations, activating the currents of Heaven over earth. We bind the works of the enemy and release the blessing of God through the words of our mouths (Mt 18:18).

"Create in us a pure heart, O God, and renew a right, persevering and steadfast spirit within us (Ps 51:10). Oh God, set a watch over our mouths and keep the door of our lips prepared to speak Your inerrant truth which brings Your light and life into dark and desperate situations (Ps 141:3). Purify us in this hour to declare Your goodness and love.

"You have taken back the keys from the evil one and possess *all* authority in Heaven and on Earth (Mt 28:18). May this key of declaring Your Word never lay dormant in our mouths, but fill us with Your grace to unlock the legacy of Your Kingdom here and now.

Amen."

> *"When you know it is God, you can stand on His Word. You don't know how it's going to happen, but you can stand on that Word."* — Betty

***

> *"I read the Word of God like I am standing right in the middle of the scroll."* — Emily

***

> *"Wow, the Bible is a great weapon! I decided to seek truth and pray the Word of God, seeking deeper and deeper revelation."* — Karli

***

Notes
1. Proverbs 31:26
2. A.W. Tozer, *The Pursuit of God: The Human Thirst for the Divine* (Wingspread Publishers, 2007), 70

CHAPTER 4

Listening & Speaking – Prophetic Prayer

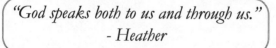

> *"God speaks both to us and through us."*
> *- Heather*

A young mother sat quietly nursing her baby in the back row of a small church. As if by some unseen hand she was suddenly propelled to her feet and forcefully downloaded a succinct message to an unsuspecting congregation.

"Now is the time to forgive. Any of you who are holding unforgiveness in your hearts, let it go!"

Then, just as abruptly, the same invisible force plunked her into her seat again. She appeared as surprised and shaken by the interruption as everyone else.

This was my introduction to the prophetic. Up until that moment, I had never heard a prophetic word given either corporately or privately. This demonstration in no way met the qualifications the Bible speaks about, **"for their strengthening, encouraging and comfort"** (1 Cor 14:3).

Until then, the morning service had progressed as per custom.

Now, however, the pastor sat in stunned silence, scanning his mind for the appropriate protocol to follow after such a sharp intrusion of the service. After what seemed like hours instead of seconds, to everyone's relief, he restored continuum to the Sunday morning liturgy.

The next day, however, he phoned the young woman apologizing for not seizing the opportunity to greater advantage. The precision and spear-like accuracy of God's word shocked him into momentary silence. She, of course, had no foreknowledge of the internal church struggles he was dealing with. Neither did she need to know.

God used a willing and available vessel to speak through that morning and many other times thereafter. Fortunately, most words God gives aren't near as weighty, but nonetheless, every bit as surgically precise.

Whether God's words are

directive or corrective,

comforting or confronting,

warning or reassuring,

detailed or vague,

He alone knows the exact meaning, purpose, and implications for today and the future of each prophetic utterance.

In that instance, God's present word for the congregation was to be spoken quickly and powerfully. It proved accurate and eventually did bring substantial change to the little congregation.

At other times, the Holy Spirit might direct the prophetic voice to brood over the word God gives for a while, incubating the fertile eggs of truth through prayer, and hatching them out in silence. More frequently, however, God speaks to those with open ears, instructing His sensitive listeners to then declare what He has spoken to those in need of **"strengthening, encouraging and comfort."**

Thankfully, that wasn't the last time God gave this woman a specific word for either an individual or a group of people. The godly insights she has spoken to me personally have been strategic and perfectly timed.

I am also grateful the severity of that first message was not the continuum of all prophetic words I have witnessed. Although, at times, that element has been present. From that first experience with the prophetic, God has made it clear to me that prophetic utterances are a gift of His grace to those He dearly loves.

> *"The prophetic speaks into the future either pulling it into existence today or compelling people to move into their destiny. When prophetic words are spoken, things change." — Patrick*

Personal Perspectives

Jan was still a child when she first began to experience prophetic intercession.

"My father died when I was ten years old. Every night while my mother sat drinking alcohol, I would go into her bedroom, praying into the night until she came in and told me to go to bed. The prophetic began during those prayer times.

"One night, I was crying and praying at the window for people who didn't know Jesus yet. Suddenly, I saw a vision of a girl being attacked. The Lord showed me the exact car and street corner of the assault. I saw in the vision a man trying to pull her into his vehicle and knew that he would rape her. I wept as I prayed intensely. Though I wanted to go and help, the Lord told me that it wouldn't be safe.

"The next morning as my mother was listening to the radio, I heard them describe the events I had seen in prayer. Again, I cried as I heard how the neighbors were woken by a voice saying, 'Wake up!' They went outside, saving and protecting the girl. The man had also been caught. Even though I rarely listened to the radio, God made sure I knew that He had intervened because of prayer.

"As a child, I learned what an honor it was to be led by God in prayer. I knew that by praying in the Spirit God could do anything as He guided my prayers.

"That was the first time I remember hearing God through a vision; it was the beginning of my journey of prophetic intercession. Time and again, He would wake me up in the night to pray.

"He was training me in intercession. I willingly said, 'Please use me. Wake me up.' "

"God's voice is pretty clear; it isn't loud, but it is always clear. Sometimes it is the quiet voice of the Spirit speaking with wisdom." — Jewell

Heather moves with aprophetic edge in all she does.

"When we prophesy over people, it is a form of prayer. We listen to God, then speak the word from Him to someone else. I didn't purposefully seek to exercise the gift of prophecy; it came so subtly. The prophetic didn't begin on a certain day but rather wove its way in after spending time with God.

"On my birthday, I was in the prayer center desiring more than anything else to meet with God. 'All I ask for my birthday is You. I know You and love Your Presence. Time please stand still, so that I can stay in this place with You.'

"I woke up a couple of days later knowing that something was different. Before this, I had constantly felt like something around my throat was trying to choke me. Though not physically, but emotionally, there had been something like invisible hands around my throat all the time. I didn't fully realize it until the feeling was gone. I knew that I had experienced deliverance.

"My only prayer had been, 'I just want Your Presence. I want to spend this day with You.' Out of that prayer, a wonderful transaction with God came. He is so good!

"God gives His rhema word—an utterance either individually or collectively spoken through the Holy Spirit and based on theology. We need to listen carefully to these rhema words, asking Him questions and seeking confirmation.

"When I'm interceding and declaring, I am speaking from Kingdom authority, proclaiming God's Word and refusing to mess with the devil or his crap.

"Recently, I saw in the spirit six to eight gray marble statues. They were like little children ten to twelve years old, each touching a flower to their chest. God said, 'These are memorials I have erected in Heaven to people's childhood. I don't forget their suffering, but erect memorials, just like you do on Earth.'

"God showed me that He validates and honors our journeys. He remembers our suffering with compassion. When we affirm people through love, patience, and time poured into their lives, they can move forward. When God gives us a prophetic word for someone, we have the authority to pray through it, speaking it out.

"Recently, a girl attended our community group for the first time. I received a prophetic word for her during worship. I said, 'Every time you stand up to worship you get shot down. You are in a new season and are going to do something new.' We gathered around her speaking many prophetic words over her.

"We didn't know that she was fatigued from the enemy's attacks, decided to quit school and had already given away her tuition. She sat there weeping as in prophetic prayer those assignments were broken off her life. As a result, it was a huge pivotal point for her and she is still at school. God put his finger on her pain and nailed it!

"God has given us the sword of His prophetic word. By declaring it, we have authority over each other, because we are part of the same family."

Emmanuel says,

"God desires to instruct and direct us. When we take time to ask God what He wants to say and do in each situation, we open our hearts to hear from Holy Spirit. Then we can prophetically speak out what we have heard. Agreeing in prayer with God produces the greatest results and the best fruit.

"My prayer journey started with a to-do-list. I still go to God with things, but I stop more and wrestle with the Lord asking Him about them. Then I keep a written record about the promises I hear Him give about those situations. When there doesn't seem to be an answer to prayer, I say, 'Lord, You have spoken to me about this. I'm holding You to Your word!'

"Most often, God speaks to me personally through thoughts and impressions, but when I'm prophesying over someone else, He usually speaks through pictures and visions. Part of the prophetic involves receiving and speaking words of knowledge. The Bible is a reliable filter for all the prophetic because it is unchangeable truth. Prophecy always lines up with it. If a prophecy is contrary to His Word, it isn't God.

"It's beneficial to test the prophetic and words of knowledge with other Christians. They will be honest and tell us if we're on target or not. It's important to walk with those who love and support us enough to help us on our spiritual journey. God isn't interested in us waking up tomorrow and becoming the next great whatever. He is interested in our journey, bringing us through different seasons. His heart is to be in partnership with us.

"Because I don't always know if it's God's voice, there is an element of faith involved in prophecy.

"When a child is growing up, its parents tell the child every-thing, 'Do this . . . do that . . . don't go there.' By being in a relationship with the Lord, abiding with Him in my heart, I don't need a prophetic word for everything. I will know that this person needs healing, that person needs encouragement, someone else a prophetic word or another a word of knowl-edge.

> *In prayer, we are partnering with Heaven to release the will of God, His Kingdom and His domain on earth.*

"God tells us what to speak prophetically out of our rela-tionship with Him as we discover His heart more."

On several occasions, I've led worship dance segments with chil-dren. One of my favorite exercises incorporates prophetic worship movement. Sometimes I ask one child to sit in the middle of a circle and have the other children pray quietly for a moment asking God to give them a prophetic word for the person in the middle. Then instead of speaking, we dance out in prophetic intercession what we feel God is saying to them. Afterward, if children were confident enough, they could share what they felt God said.

Here are just a few examples children spoke during one of these exercises:

- "I felt the word 'courage.' I think God is telling you that you are stronger than you think. He has big plans for you."
- "I saw seeds. I think that you find the good seeds in people's hearts and share the glory of Jesus with them."
- "I think you are like a forest of big strong trees. You are very strong."
- "I felt like God was filling your heart with splatters of love and grace. He was breathing happiness into your life."
- "I felt like there was a big problem at school, but God says, 'Get together with other kids who know Jesus because the solution will come as you get together like a team.'"
- "I saw you are like a lion—beautiful, poised, perfect and brave."

It would often surprise me how consistent the words would be for each child. Like the colors of light reflecting off a diamond, God's word to His young children came in different ways but with a common theme. The things they said were always encouraging, expressing love and value.

"We need to give people safe places to hear God's voice and share it. One of the biggest problems is that people are afraid to step out and share what they are hearing from God."
— Keegan

Merodee said,

"Before I got married, came home and started having children, I forgot about contending for a life of prayer. More than I realized, I believed answering prayer was something God did in the past, not now. I still prayed, but not at regular intervals or as a discipline. They were more needs-based, survival-type prayers.

"Though it sounds harsh, prayer was fairly manipulative. I was praying to control people and situations instead of bringing myself into submission to the Spirit and the Word. Because I exchanged the intimacy of prayer for the tool of prayer, I was lonely and grew spiritually hard.

"When I was pregnant with our daughter, I started hemorrhaging at six weeks. It was then that I identified with the pattern of contending for life. She was born at twenty-eight weeks, weighing two pounds five ounces. She couldn't breathe on her own and was on a ventilator. We had been given powerful prophetic words and dreams that encouraged us during that time. As her parents, we knew that we were responsible for contending for her life through prayer.

> *New ceilings require new levels of prayer.*

"We constantly prayed the Word of God over her—prayers of faith and contending. Nonetheless, I struggled to believe why God allowed this to happen and didn't know if I could fully trust Him. I was honestly afraid to come close to Him. My prayers came out of a desire to control circumstances more than out of intimacy with Him.

"I learned a lot about being strengthened in the Lord while at the same time being catapulted in faith through the trial. It was an invitation to grow deeper in intimacy with God.

"I knew that to come close to Him, I would have to lay down my pride and strength. I was terrified that if I did, everything would fall apart. God didn't give up on me, however."

God gave Yoge prophetic words that He used to bring her unbelieving members of her family to Himself.

"There were many times I would kneel in prayer, feeling full of fire. I didn't always understand what God was doing. While in prayer, God gave me a vision of my uncle with dark circles around his eyes. I stopped praying and said to my dad, 'Do you know why nothing is going well with your business? Your own brother has done black magic on you.' Then, I continued to pray, 'I bind this in the Name of Jesus.' Immediately after that prayer, my father's business started doing well and my dad became a believer in Jesus. He knew that when I prayed to Jesus things would go well.

"When I see these things through a vision, I know I need to take it seriously and pray. If I say that Jesus is here, people look at me like I'm crazy, but when I tell them something specific about their life, they begin to cry and know that God is real.

"There was a woman who came to church and wanted the pastors to pray for her. I felt irritated and knew that something wasn't right. I said to her, 'Yesterday you went to the temple to worship an idol and now you come here today!' My pastor was surprised because she had been a Christian for many years. He looked at me like I said something wrong. 'No!' I said, 'This lady went to the temple. I can feel the irritation in my spirit. Tell her to go away and ask for forgiveness. Then she can come to church.' The pastor also received confirmation in his spirit while I was speaking. The woman started to cry and admitted she had gone to the temple the day before.

"Up until that time, my mom believed that everything was god, every supernatural power was god, the moon and the sun were gods. But when she witnessed these things, she came to know that the One I worshipped was the only God.

"After my mother and father were saved, my grandfather had a problem at the temple where he was working as an employee. When he came to our house, I didn't know that he had just lost his job at the temple. I said, 'Your job is done at the temple.

'You need to come back to Jesus because you're old. I don't want you to go to hell.' He asked how I knew he lost his job. I told him, 'When I was praying, God showed me that today your job is done. That's the reason why you came home now.' Because of that word from God, my grandfather began to pray to Jesus, was saved and baptized."

Unlocking the Legacy

The Word of God is complete—without anything to be added or taken away. Yet, at the same time, God hasn't suddenly become silent. He continues to speak, encouraging and strengthening the body of Christ, as He brings her to perfection. God speaks clearly. We, on the other hand, often have difficulty hearing and responding to Him.

Paul instructed the Corinthian church,

> **"Follow the way of love and eagerly desire gifts of the Spirit, especially prophecy. For anyone who speaks in a tongue does not speak to people but to God. Indeed, no one understands them; they utter mysteries by the Spirit. But the one who *prophesies* speaks to people for their *strengthening, encouraging and comfort*. Anyone who speaks in a tongue edifies themselves, but the one who prophesies edifies the church. I would like every one of you to speak in tongues, but I would rather have you prophesy."**
> **1 Corinthians 14:1-5**
> **(Emphasis mine)**

The prophetic is primarily received through seeing and hearing. Seers often experience God's voice through dreams, visions or imagery; hearers are more tuned to God's voice through the Bible, audible words, thoughts and impressions. Those who function in the prophetic usually experience a combination of both these streams.

Prophetic intercession is the ability to hear and see the

intentions of God, pray it back to Him and declare it over others. It's the ability to catch the stirring of God's heart and then unite with Him by speaking on His behalf. A strong vein of the progressive revelation of God's love flows through prophetic intercession.

> *"We are not just human beings, but prophetic beings already linked to Heaven. I try to stay in tune with God to catch whatever He is doing to see His will done on Earth." — Karli*

In this way, the Holy Spirit stirs us to pray for situations and circumstances we have little or no knowledge about. Through prophetic intercession, we pray *with* God rather than *to* God.

Listening and speaking require waiting in God's Presence, reading the Scriptures and making ourselves available to hear His heartbeat. Prophetic intercession never originates with man, but is from God, with God and by God's grace and power. Sometimes it will be spoken through redeclaration of Scripture, giving warnings, claiming His promises, or proclaiming His desire. Our prayerful petitions come into agreement with what God has already spoken or shown us.

Perhaps the greatest illustration of prophetic intercession comes from Daniel. He **"understood from the Scriptures, according to the word of the LORD given to Jeremiah the prophet, that the desolation of Jerusalem would last seventy years"** (Dn 9:2). Daniel read the Word and caught God's heart. He understood that the punishment of the nation was limited to seventy years, and those seventy years had expired.

> **"So I turned to the Lord God and pleaded with him in prayer and petition, in fasting, and in sackcloth and ashes."**
> **Daniel 9:3**

Daniel didn't see the promise as his ticket out of Babylon. He prayed and petitioned for what God had promised to come to pass. Daniel knew that what God had spoken would happen only when someone took His word seriously and prayed it through bringing relief to His people. Daniel picked up the challenge, appealing to God's faithfulness to His promise.

"Lord, listen! Lord, forgive!
Lord, hear and act!
For your sake, my God, do not delay . . ."
Daniel 9:19

Prophetic intercession unlocks the path for the fulfillment of divine promises. These promises come to fruition when the Holy Spirit speaks to human vessels who proclaim the divine word before God's throne. Like with Daniel, it may be the written Word of God; at other times it might be a word spoken through the Holy Spirit into an explicit situation or for a specific person's life.

God's promise was sealed in the Book of Jeremiah until Daniel recognized it as a key to unlocking the legacy for his nation's freedom from exile. With confidence, he spoke God's Word back to Him, "God, You said! I'm claiming Your promise!"

There is within every prophetic promise something hidden until it is verbally expressed back to God. God taps His intercessors on the shoulder, making them aware of His heart, stirring them to pray for a specific thing in a strategic moment. With the Word, God gives faith and direct instruction.

Sometimes we might be stirred to pray at great length with fasting like Daniel. However, most of the time, we position ourselves to daily hear and receive His fresh, living word. Then we can write it out, pray it through and step out in faith doing whatever God calls us to do.

"Not all intercessors are prophets,
but all prophets are intercessors!"

Jeremiah says, **"But if they are prophets, and if the word of the LORD is with them, let them now make intercession to the LORD of hosts. . ."** (27:18 NKJV). The goal of operating in a prophetic gift is to combine it with intercessory prayer.

An employee on emergency call twenty-four hours a day, seven days a week, must continually be ready for the next appointment. He never knows when he will be called into duty or the length of the shift he must serve. His only responsibility is to be ready when the call comes.

Prophetic intercession is similar. It is up to us to develop a continuous God-consciousness and willingness to be interrupted by Him for His purposes. As we grow in intercession we will become more certain of God's timing and process in each situation. One of the greatest obstacles to prophetic intercession may very well be the vulnerable willingness needed to allow God to intercede through us in ways we don't understand or necessarily feel comfortable with.

There are two main avenues through which prophetic intercession flows. The first is interceding to God on behalf of others like Abraham did over Sodom and Gomorrah (Gn 18:16-33) or Moses with the people of Israel (Ps 106:23). The second involves taking a stand against enemy attacks, as David did before Goliath (1 Sm 17).

> **"I looked for someone among them who would**
> **build up the wall and stand before me in the gap on**
> **behalf of the land so I would not have to**
> **destroy it, but I found no one."**
> **Ezekiel 22:30**

Whether God calls us to pray for a foreign missionary, a condition we don't naturally know exists, or an individual we have no close relationship with, prophetic intercession requires a level of trusting God. However, operating in the prophetic is one strategic key to unlocking legacy. It is listening, watching and speaking forth what God desires. Prophetic intercession is God-initiated, God-inspired, and God-directed utterances.

Taking Territory

"Lord give us a Samuel heart that willingly says, **'Speak, LORD, for your servant is listening'** (1 Sm 3:7-11). We want to discern Your voice from the voices of others and to speak Your message with pinpoint accuracy even when it isn't a message of soft pillows, pretty rainbows or abundant provision.

"Lord, as we seek to hear Your voice, we refuse to allow anything You say silently **'fall to the ground'** unspoken when, where, how and to whom You desire. May we be recognized as Your prophets as You continue to appear to us, revealing Yourself to us through Your word (1 Sm 3:19-21).

"O Lord, may these words ring true for each of us. Give us the grace to hear, the courage to speak, and the will to obey.

"Thank You for the key of prophetic intercession with which You are exposing the secret strategies of the enemy,

giving clear direction and insight to the saints,

declaring Your heart to the world,

drawing many into the Kingdom of God,

and bringing Your will to all people.

"Like Anna we choose to never leave Your Presence **'but (worship) night and day, fasting and praying.'** So that in the right moment we will speak, giving **'thanks (to) God'** and showing Jesus to all who will listen (Lk 2:36-38).

"We ask for increased sensitivity to both the written Word and the nudging of the Holy Spirit. May human reasoning never impede either our prayers or boldly sharing what You put on our hearts. Your Word is truth. We praise You, Lord, because **'not one word has failed of all the good promises'** that You have given (1Kgs 8:56).

"We are posted as intercessory watchmen upon the borders of our families, communities and nation. We will not be silent, as we stand in the gap against enemy attack, but will speak as You direct. We call upon You Lord—remembering, bringing into mind, recollecting, mentioning, meditating upon, marking down and recording, and retaining in our thoughts all You have spoken.[2] Rouse us from apathy and indifference (Is 62:6-7).

"Give us wisdom and discernment to utilize the key of prophetic intercession with authority and maturity. Thank You for this mighty tool to unlock our legacy and the legacies of many others.

"But we ask, Lord, that You would ignite prophetic intercession in this hour like never before. Raise it up, Lord! Awaken the heart of intercessors who have become discouraged and battle-worn. Infuse them again with divine insight and prophetic utterance. May they be bold as lions, with eyes of eagles seeing into the spirit realm, possessing divine wisdom and tact. Train up an army of new prophetic intercessors circling the wall with valor. Yes, Lord, equip these powerful keyholders as they unlock the legacy of thousands.

Amen."

"God speaks through a thought, Scriptures or pictures. I am learning and becoming more discerning of His voice, His character and personality, as well as how He interacts with me personally." – Joy-Lyn

***

"When I know God's voice in my private times, I hear His voice more easily when I'm listening for others."
– Charlene S.

***

"Prophetically God speaks to me. My spirit gets an impression and I suddenly understand better, or I will get a picture." – Amanda C.

***

Notes

1. Cindy Jacobs, *The Voice of God: How God Speaks Personally and Corporately to His Children Today* (Ventura, Regal Books, 1982), 38.
2. Warren Baker, D.R.E and Eugene Carpenter, Ph.D., ed., *Complete Word Study Dictionary: Old Testament: For a Deeper Understanding of The Word* (Chattanooga, AMG Publishers, 2003), 2142.

CHAPTER 5

A Time to Deliver
– Travailing Prayer

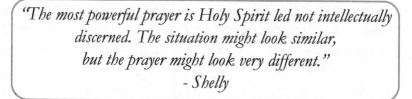

*"The most powerful prayer is Holy Spirit led not intellectually
discerned. The situation might look similar,
but the prayer might look very different."*
- Shelly

Kneeling with his face to the floor, he wailed. Great heaves and moans emulated from deep within him like wordless groans of anguish. A sadness and travail possessed him with heartbreaking agony.

"Jesus . . . oh, Jesus . . . oh, my God . . ." Every word was strained, ebbing from a breathless whisper to a painful wail, as he entered into God's Presence with weapons of prayer unformed by human hands.

Hour after hour, he kept vigil until the floor pooled with tears. His chest throbbed as if his heart was being pulled sinew by sinew from his body. Morning, noon and night the burden for lost souls, those who did not yet know the Lord, pressed heavily upon him.

As the first Christian in his family, he was ostracized for his faith by his father, mother, sister, brother, and spouse. But the pain of rejection and alienation by those he loved mattered little in comparison to the great weight he felt in travailing prayer for the spiritually lost who were still living their lives apart from God.

It wasn't just his family he interceded for, but also for his neighbors, community, and nation. His prayers extended to unknown people groups spanning the globe. Whoever God pressed upon his heart, he lifted back to Him, calling for repentance—waging war for souls to be snatched from hell's dark chasm and presented at Heaven's open gate.

Alone and unseen by any human eye, he fought the battle for souls. He believed beyond a doubt that Jesus Christ gave His life for these, and as such, was worthy of receiving all He died to redeem.

At other times his travail traversed spiritual domains to
provoke prodigals homeward,
eradicate physical illness from the diseased,
blast spiritual blindness from the deceived,
mend relationships long broken, or
speak peace to the mentally tormented.

Sometimes taking territory and unlocking legacy isn't the casual, comfortable, complacent prayer of distant ones. Travail is the prayerful groanings for lives that are broken, hearts that are bleeding and souls that are lost. Travail never originates from the will or emotion of mankind, but rather descends from above. Travailing prayer births forth the seed of truth conceived and carried within the heart of the intercessor.

Yet, this young man's prayers, like ours, is but a fraction of the intercession Jesus prayed in the garden long ago.

"My soul is overwhelmed with sorrow to the point of death . . . Going a little farther, he fell with his face to the ground and prayed, 'My Father, if it is possible, may this cup be taken from me . . .' Then he returned to his disciples and found them sleeping. 'Couldn't you men keep watch with me for one hour?' He asked . . . 'Watch and pray . . . The spirit is willing, but the flesh is weak.' He went a second time and prayed . . ."
Matthew 26:36-46; Mark 14:32-42

Jesus' prayers were so intense that "**an angel from Heaven appeared to him and strengthened him. And being in anguish, he prayed more earnestly, and his sweat was like drops of blood falling to the ground**" *(*Lk 22:43-44*)*.

Though Luke had left his medical practice, trading in the tools of his trade for the sandals of a disciple, his concern for Jesus during His great travail could not be dismissed. Who but Jesus intercedes like this? No one! Only here does the Bible record Jesus travailing in this manner and never again would anyone intercede to this extent.

Personal Perspectives

Helen said,

"Quite often, I would be moved with an overwhelming urge to pray for an individual. It was almost like God was telling me before someone died.

"One day, I was making my bed when suddenly I thought about my nephew being hurt. I immediately started praying for him. A few minutes later my mother-in-law phoned asking me to pray because he had been in an accident. I thought, 'God is way ahead of you.'

"Another night, I had this overwhelming urge to pray for my elderly great-aunt. Even though I hadn't seen her for years, I began to plead for her salvation. A couple of days later, as my Dad was leaving after a visit, he said, 'Oh yes! I wanted to tell you, your great-aunt died.'

"I believe God shows us things so we will intercede for people's souls. There were many times God had me pray for seniors in the community in this way. When I sense somebody doesn't know God, I feel an urgency to pray for their salvation.

> *I need to be listening to the Holy Spirit*
> *so I can be more effective in prayer.*

"I wonder how many people get into Heaven on their death bed because someone prayed and interceded in their last moments of life. God isn't going to stir you to pray for something that won't bear fruit. Only Heaven will reveal how prayer changed people's eternal existence.

"In prayer, we become co-laborers with God, praying with Him. How exciting is that! We may think we should pray for someone, but real prayer is God moving in us to pray for people."

God stirred Amanda [C.] to intercede during critical moments in the lives of others.

"Intercession was a word I had heard but didn't have a grid for. Up to this point, I would talk to God and pray in tongues a little.

"One of my housemates had worked in Alaska with a fellow who would sometimes come over to our place. I didn't like him and thought he should leave. One night when he wasn't over, I felt this crushing weight on me. I was flat on my face weeping and praying in tongues for about forty-five minutes. Afterward, I wondered what had happened and thought, 'God, how often are You going to do this?' Later, I found out that he had been planning on committing suicide that night, but didn't. I knew then why I had been praying for him.

"That same year I received an email from my cousin who was dealing with depression. She was desperate and asking for prayer. Again, I found myself weeping and praying for her intensely. I looked up and saw a strip of light reflect off a spider web in my room. God spoke to me that there was a glimmer of hope. That prompting became the subject of a painting. I used the primary colors together to form mostly black, then added a strip of light to the picture. Since then, God has used the painting to bring hope to others. It has been passed around to various people going through dark times.

"I want to learn more about intercession. I'm not afraid to get messy, whether it is through intense weeping, praying in tongues, or repentance. At times for me, intercession can also include painting, dancing, groanings, or however else God leads.

"At one point, it felt like almost everyone in my prayer circle had stepped back from prayer, but I still had a strong sense of revival for our city and our church and wanted to be a part of it. The Book of Revelation talks about bowls being filled with people's prayers and being tipped out (Rev 5:8). I believe that the bowl over our city has been filled with the prayers of faithful people.

"One time I was sitting in the prayer room by myself praying for revival. For about a year, I had been praying the Scriptures in 1 Kings 18 about Elijah and Mount Carmel over our city and church. I asked, 'God, when is this going to happen? Why do I need to keep praying?'

"God showed me that there had been other people before me who had prayed without seeing the answer. Elijah prayed too and kept on praying for rain, without seeing results. Finally, a little wisp of cloud appeared (1 Kgs 18:41-46). In the same way, birthing a revival requires consistency in prayer."

Jan shared several illustrations showing how God speaks prophetically to her. God's prophetic word combined with prayer has impacted many lives as a result.

"I was teaching a class on prayer and prophetic intercession and sensed God was going to do something different among us. Soon after, someone new came to the prayer center. We only had a brief opportunity to welcome her because one of the intercessors was immediately burdened, praying in tongues and travailing in prayer. After I explained to the new-comer what was happening, she immediately recognized that she carried the same burden. Intercessors must have the godly character to sustain prayer to breakthrough. Prophetic inter-cession and travail also need a safe place of expression.

"Week after week, God spoke to us and through us in many different ways, allowing us to continue to release our burdens while giving us an understanding of how to pray effective-ly through different situations. We learned to discern the Lord's voice and understand what the Lord wanted us to do and to know His timing. 'Is the time right now? God, what are You telling us to do?'

"This new woman in our prayer group had an estranged daughter to whom she hadn't spoken to for many years. Her daughter, who had become a prostitute, had tried to commit suicide several times. We felt we were to spend all weekend in fasting and prayer, sensing that God would bring the break-through. We wrote down specific words God gave us and then we continued to wait on God in faith.

"On the following Monday, this woman received a call from her daughter. Because of the different Scriptures and stories God had highlighted to us, we already knew what was going to happen.

"We blessed this woman to go and see her daughter, but first, she needed to walk through forgiveness. God softened and healed her heart as day after day she forgave at ever-deepening levels.

"This woman's daughter ended up coming to our prayer meeting and, as a group, we led her to the Lord. She was baptized in the

Holy Spirit and continued to join us in prayer. It was amazing to have her with us. This salvation and breakthrough launched us into more prayer initiatives."

Allison shared,

"The grace of God has helped me to embrace diverse seasons of prayer. At present, I'm consistently bringing people's needs to the Lord, through petition and praying Scriptures.

"Just last night, I was grieved and prayed with travail and groanings in the Spirit for the situation and people in a Middle Eastern country. With what is going on in the world, I feel a lot of grief and heaviness—not from the enemy, but from a broken heart. I cried out for God's intervention, 'Oh Lord, we are so desperate and need You.'

"In burden-bearing prayer, I feel the pain of others. Many times, the weight we feel in prayer is not our issue. We must ask the Lord from where the sense of heaviness or scattered feeling is coming. We may be sensing God's burden for individuals, people groups or nations. Intercessory prayer releases the burden back to the Lord with or without a sense of travailing for hours.

"My prayer is, 'Lord give us a soft heart to receive those burdens.'

> *Simple acts of faith in travailing prayer come from a sensitive and soft heart able to receive the burden of others.*

"Galatians 6:2 tells us to **'carry each other's burdens, and in this way . . . fulfill the law of Christ.'** In burden-bearing prayer, picking up and carrying the burdens of others, there is no room for personal pride. Travailing prayer reminds me that I am in partnership with the Holy Spirit, releasing Him to move in the lives of others."

For Karli, birthing or travailing prayer has come for brief seasons.

"I have stepped into intercession for different things in different seasons. It's a type of prayer that I don't have nailed down yet and am just learning. One example would be interceding for a few girls at work who didn't have the energy to do their jobs. They were feeling weighed down by worry, anxiety and depression.

"God shows us when He wants push-through prayer, not from our strength but prayer He initiates, where His power comes on us to speak His word through us. Travailing prayer brings break-throughs by waiting on God to fill our prayers with power."

Travail was a foreign word for Kate. It took her a while to figure out what God was doing through her.

"I didn't understand when the Holy Spirit began moving in me through travail and intense weeping that I couldn't stop. It began when a few of us gathered together for prayer.

"I had no clue what was going on. I didn't ask and wouldn't have asked God for that kind of moving of Holy Spirit in my life. I didn't even know the term 'intercessor.' God sovereignly brought that travail upon me. I had no control over travailing prayer; I was just trying to figure out how to work with God in it.

"Pursuing the way Holy Spirit was moving in me became a huge learning curve. I read *Rees Howells: Intercessor*. I bawled buckets as I read it and I couldn't put it down. To some degree, I understood this man's life and the Holy Spirit's moving in Him. I gained more understanding about intercessory prayer, as well.

"The word intercessor implies such a mantle. Though other people said that about me, I never said that about myself for a long time. There have been periods when that mantle has been more intense in certain ways or types of prayer than I am presently experiencing.

> *Jesus Christ is the Lord of prayer. It is completely His doing. We move hand in hand with Him in our calling to pray.*

"Through travailing prayer, I have seen salvations, healings, deliverances, and the conviction of Holy Spirit, as well as many changes in people's lives and circumstances. I have also experienced a deepening in my walk with the Lord as a result of intercession. Jesus Christ being formed in the lives of individuals through travail is an incredible by-product of intercession.

"There's a breaker anointing which comes with travail, allowing God to break through whatever is going on in the spirit realm that is not of Him or pleasing to Him. Many times, I have seen Him break through that kind of garbage, aligning someone with Himself.

"Holy Spirit prays through us in many different ways. The things He accomplishes in and through people, individually and corporately, is amazing.

"The Lord lets us know that He is laughing at the enemy when He releases laughter in prayer. When God laughs at the enemy, it's a sign that the victory is won and He's dealt with the oppression. He says to the enemy, 'Get lost! Why do you even bother me? I am the Lion of Judah. Come into alignment with My will in this situation.'

> *Victory is ours! It is done!*

"God may give us words to decree and declare through intercession or there may be an outburst of joy and laughter. Intercession can be intense and no demon is going to mess with it. Human mouths are shut as God exercises His perfect will and sovereignty in situations. That excites me!

"Holy Spirit is amazing. We praise and worship God for His Almightiness. Prayer is so multifaceted; the life of prayer is exciting. No one can put God in a box."

Sharon has carried the burden of intercession often. She shared,

"God gives us compassion as the Holy Spirit moves through us with weeping. Instead of words, we weep and travail as a river of life flows out of us. **'We do not know what we ought to pray for, but the Spirit himself intercedes for us through wordless groans'** (Rom 8:26-27).

"Who can define intercessory prayer or what God does? I know what it is for me, but I can't explain it in words. It's a mystery—communion with God, but more.

> *Travail is the Lord birthing life through prayer.*

"Jesus said, **'My house will be called a house of prayer'** (Mt 21:13). He didn't say it should be a house of preaching or teaching. Prayer is of the utmost importance to Him.

"To see God come with His glory is not like turning on a switch. We need to get on our faces and pray. Prayer is work! The enemy fights tooth and nail against prayer. In many places, prayer has almost been shut down for a season, but God is raising prayer up again.

"In past revivals, we have seen the result of people abandoning themselves to prayer, as saints fasted and prayed in desperation. We don't hold a candle to them. Through their prayers, even people walking down the street were convicted by the Holy Spirit and children moved around in the church services praying for people.

"I pray, 'Do it again, Lord.' "

Karin said,

"Though I didn't study prayer, I developed in prayer further when I moved into a home with two powerful intercessors. These women had such a humble way of praying, as they stayed in a place of mercy and trusted God to intervene. One of the big keys for intercessory prayer is knowing God is kind and merciful. He doesn't desire anyone to miss what He has for them.

"An intercessor can't afford to be critical in prayer. God gives us peace to even pray for our worst enemies or abusers. When the heart of an intercessor aligns with God's heart of compassion, a new level of freedom in prayer is attained. Intercessory prayer doesn't condone evil but desires to see people set free. Travailing prayer seeks God's grace rather than His punishment."

Charlene talked about another important but often overlooked aspect of intercession and travail.

"When we moved to a new community, I encountered people praying with authority. I realized they weren't just making requests to God but were praying Scripture and applying it to the need. I hadn't heard people pray like that before, but I knew it was important.

"Within a short time, I saw someone travailing in prayer and walked over to where she was. Another woman told me to put my hand on her back to help her, like a midwife, protecting her as she was praying. After she received the breakthrough, I went home. My spirit understood this type of prayer, but my mind didn't.

"Later, I called her and asked, 'Can you tell me what that was?'

"She said, 'Travailing in the Spirit.'

"She named it without actually answering my question. She suggested that I read books on intercession. To her, birthing things in prayer was nothing extraordinary but normal.

> *Intercession is not something you make happen. You can't start travail and you can't stop it either.*

"I was beginning to recognize that prayer was more significant than I previously thought. I hadn't been in an atmosphere before with that kind of culture for prayer.

"After that, I just hung out with people who were praying. Holy Spirit mentored me through watching. I read a few books on prayer and although they were awesome books about praying in faith, how to pray lists, being faithful and stewarding the things God gives you to pray for, I knew they weren't feeding my spirit or teaching me what I needed to know.

"Exhaustion is a hindrance to prayer which we need to address. We have to be shrewd with our bodies; it's hard to pray when we're tired. If prayer is a priority, perhaps we need to take a nap to be fresh and ready at prayer time. Does prioritizing prayer mean we need to say 'no' to other things so we aren't too tired to pray? At times, fatigue may be a spiritual attack we can pray through, but if we are called to prayer, we need to steward our lives so we are fresh to pray.

"Sometimes we spiritualize prayer so much it isn't practical. Yes, there are things we are responsible for, but we have to be far-sighted and wise.

> *If the enemy can keep us from doing anything,*
> *he will keep us from praying.*

"Reading your Bible is great, but it is not the same as praying:
   prayer changes you first;
         prayer changes the world around you;
               prayer changes your community;
                     prayer changes eternal destinies.

"I needed to physically train my body for prayer by going to the gym and losing some weight. Sometimes prayer can be intense. Travail is physically hard on your body, so we need to do our best to be healthy to pray.

"I know there are people who are waiting for their healing; its difficult to pray when we're hurting or physically in pain. Even in that place, we can say, 'Devil you may have put this sickness on me and I'm not healed yet, but I'm still going to pray. I may not be able to get up and do this or that, but I'm going to pray until my last breath.' "

85

Unlocking the Legacy

Everything physically changes within a woman in the process of conception and nurturing a new life within her. Her body will be forever changed as she gives herself for the life of another. Though each woman's experience and response to the birthing process can be quite different, all must labor to deliver that new life.

The purpose of travail, both naturally and spiritually, is to bring forth life—a life not conceived on our own. During natural and spiritual birthing, the focus is not on the travail, but rather on the new life being brought into the Kingdom. Especially regarding prayer, the emphasis should not be on what occurs outwardly, but rather on what God is doing.

Though many people I interviewed experienced some type of emotional response while travailing in prayer (such as weeping, wailing, or groaning) not everyone did or will. We cannot judge what is happening in the spirit realm by what is going on in the natural, either in this, or in any other type of prayer.

> **"In the same way, the Spirit helps us in our weak-
> ness. We do not know what we ought to pray for,
> but the Spirit himself intercedes for us through**
> *wordless groans.* **And he who searches our hearts
> knows the mind of the Spirit, because the Spirit
> intercedes for God's people in accordance
> with the will of God."**
> **Romans 8:26-27**
> **(Emphasis mine)**

Jesus said that for those who believe in Him, **"rivers of living water will flow from within"** (Jn 7:38). The Greek word for "within" is *koilia*, a feminine noun for hollow, belly, stomach, or womb.[1] The Holy Spirit who resides within us desires to freely birth life through us. Birthing is a more accurate description of travailing prayer.

A woman's womb is not the source, but rather the carrier of life. Through prayer, we are the spiritual carriers intended to release the power of God, the Source of all life, to the unsaved world.

At creation, the Holy Spirit's active involvement was evident as

He hovered, birthing life out of the formless and empty darkness that covered the earth (Gn 1:1-2). Just like in the beginning, Holy Spirit desires to be released, hovering over the formless, wasted lives of those needing life, hope, vision, purpose and destiny in Christ.

In prayer, Elijah squatted in a birthing position on Mount Carmel, birthing in prayer a miraculous downpour which ended a three-year drought (I Kgs 18:41-45). Elijah was a man, no different than you or me (Jas 5:17). Yet, through his birthing prayer, brazen skies unleashed a downpour, transforming famine into feasting. Spiritual bondage over his nation was broken and multitudes declared, **"The LORD—he is God!"** Oh, how my heart cries for God to do it again!

The psalmist said that those who sow in tears will reap with songs of joy. Prayer waters the word of truth, bringing fruitful results (Ps 126:5,6). The intense travailing prayer of Jesus in the Garden of Gethsemane (Mt 26:36-45), as He was deeply troubled and overwhelmed with sorrow, continues to bring sons and daughters into God's Kingdom through spiritual rebirth (Is 66:7-8).

Like Sharon, we too can read about past revivals where people were saved, delivered, healed and restored into a right relationship with the Father before they ever entered a church service or heard a sermon. How? Travailing prayer released the Holy Spirit to hover throughout the area birthing life out of the dead, spiritually sterile landscape.

> *"Our prayers can and do cause the Holy Spirit to move into situations where He then releases His power to bring life. We do have a part in producing the hovering of the Holy Spirit . . . untold millions await t heir births into the kingdom of God."* [2]

Rather than indefinable or mystical, birthing prayer is intentional, laboring intercession for the primary purpose of the salvation of souls. Travailing prayer

brings light into the darkened realms of enemy influence,

delivers hope into a seemingly hopeless situation,

carries truth to those bound by deception,

transforms sterile ground into fruitfulness, and

breaks through chains of oppression and depression, opening the Heavens to release a spiritual flood that refreshes and brings life.

Duncan Campbell, who witnessed the revival in the Hebrides Islands, said,

> *"Suddenly a cry is heard . . . a young man burdened for*
> *the souls of his fellow-men is pouring out his soul in*
> *intercession . . . The man prayed until he collapsed and*
> *lay prostrate on the floor of the church building. The*
> *congregation, moved by a power they could not resist,*
> *came back into the church, and a wave of conviction*
> *swept over the gathering, moving strong men to*
> *cry to God for mercy."* [3]

Taking Territory

"Lord, if this is the result of travailing prayer, conceive in each of us this burden of prayer. Transform us, giving us compassionate hearts of flesh. May we be willing to become messy, even indecent, in prayer for the sake of the lost.

"Lord, in all this we are gravely aware of the importance of reaching the highest calling and greatest goal of prayer—to birth the life of Christ in our generation. The need for travail has not ended; the purpose of birthing prayer has not shifted through time.

> **'(We) have not already obtained all this, or**
> **have already arrived at (our) goal . . . (We) press on**
> **to take hold of that for which Christ Jesus took hold**
> **of (us) . . . (We) do not consider (ourselves) yet to**
> **have taken hold of it. But one thing (we) do: For-**
> **getting what is behind and straining toward what is**
> **ahead, (we) press on toward the goal . . .**
> **which God has called (us) to'**
> **(Phil 3:12-14).**

"As if apprehended by You, Lord, we desire to apprehend that for which also we are apprehended. You have called us to seize, possess and take back the territory the enemy has decimated and turned into a wilderness, birthing spiritual life again and again. Jesus, by dying, You overcame death; by rising, You gave life. Access has been purchased by Your blood and given freely to all.

"We count the cost. We are willing to pay the price necessary for the acceleration of spiritual birth among the lost and dying. We are gripped by Your grace. Destinies hang in the balance, as eternities of either Heaven or hell await.

"The enemy has had his way long enough. We have been radically transformed by the life of the Lord Jesus Christ. We cannot and will not go back to anything that limits what the Spirit of life in Christ seeks to accomplish in the lives of the people of this generation. We are on a mission to take back what the devil has stolen from the people of God in this area; to re-establish the Holy Name of the Lord in this territory, to see the spiritually desolate places bloom once again like a garden; to build back this area spiritually for a habitation to the Lord; to impact this and all nations with the Gospel of the Lord Jesus Christ. My city and nation will be a place of redemption, restoration, deliverance, healing, and hope; a place where the joy of the Lord will replace the oppression and depression in the hearts of the people and where the unrestrained worship of the Lord will be released."[4]

"For too long the thief has been able to steal, kill and destroy. Jesus, we cry out to You. May we have life, and have it to the full (Jn 10:10). Your abundant life is available to all who believe. Lord, increase our faith for

life instead of death,
adoption instead of abandonment,
freedom instead of slavery and
belonging instead of insecurity.

"Lord Jesus, **'You have the words of eternal life. We have come to believe and to know that you are the Holy One of God'** (Jn 6:68-69). We kneel before You with one request, to draw others into this same saving knowledge. We plead with unrelenting fervency for the souls of the lost, until we see life birthed in them. One by one, bring them into the Kingdom, writing their names in the Lamb's Book of Life (Rev 13:8). Take them from darkness to light, from sin's grimy pit to solid ground, from aimlessness to purposeful living.

"Raise up intercessors, Lord. Ignite those willing to fill their lamps with the oil of Your Presence, praying through the night if necessary so Your light will shine. **'Darkness covers the earth and thick darkness is over the peoples, but the LORD rises . . . his glory appears . . .'** (Is 60:2). Now is the time; today is the day of salvation. This is the time of Your favor; Your ears are tuned to our prayers asking for help (2 Cor 6:2-3).

"Just as a woman in labor has no rest until her child is delivered, we press into prayer until we see redemption spring forth in the lives of those we love. Come, Lord! Send a mighty rushing wind from Heaven, filling Your people with urgency and power to take the Gospel into every nation (Acts 2:2-4). Send tongues of fire upon us, empowering us to pray and intercede by Your Spirit, to rise and go, declaring the Good News with all who will hear and receive.

Amen."

"In intercession, I feel people's pain as my own and pray it out. I have joy praying for them. It isn't a burden and doesn't drain me." — Shelly

***

"I don't feel the big burdens to pray for hours, but the Spirit of intercession has fallen on me with fiery prayer releasing whatever God puts in my heart." — Heather

***

> *"When you walk with the Spirit, you know how much God loves people and wants to bring them freedom. His heart becomes your heart; you can't help but love too." — Caren*

***

Notes

1. Spiros Zodhiates Th.D., ed., *The Complete Word Study Dictionary: New Testament: For a Deeper Understanding of the Word*, rev. ed., (Chattanooga, AMG International Inc., 1993), 872.
2. Dutch Sheets, *Intercessory Prayer: How God Can Use Your Prayers to Move Heaven and Earth* (Ventura, Regal Books, 1996), 132.
3. Tommy Tenney, *Open Heaven: The Secret Power of a Door Keeper* (Shippensburg, Destiny Image Publishers Inc., 2012), 158-159.
4. Source unknown

CHAPTER 6

The Currents of Heaven – Creative Movement

> *"Conversation with God, or prayer, is the real meat. You pray until you start giving praise which leads to worship."*
> *– Christie*

I jumped off the running boards of the truck, rushing to move the last of the supplies into the storage shed. My foot inadvertently landed on the large round head of a post maul. The maul rolled backward with the momentum of my body, propelling me against a concrete ledge. Searing pain ran through me in nauseating currents as I lay helpless on the ground.

Upon impact, I cried, "Jesus!" Now as I lay, unable to move on the cold, dew-covered ground, His name subconsciously flowed from my trembling lips. It was harvest time. Everyone would be in the fields until well after dark; no one would be returning home any time soon. "Jesus," I whispered again as I tried to relax my breathing and assess my condition. Over and over I uttered that Name; He alone was my help.

After about half an hour, I was able to roll from my side to my knees and then edge myself a hundred meters to the house. "Can't hold up the harvest," I rationalized as I crawled toward the bathroom, filling the tub with hot water. I gently slipped in, hoping to relax my body, ease the pain and restore movement. Surging spasms uncontrollably vibrated through me. "Jesus, help!" I whispered.

My left torso downward was affected the most. When I stood to my feet to walk, my left leg was uncooperative. With each step I commanded movement. "Ankle, knee, hip . . . ankle, knee, hip . . . move in Jesus' Name . . ."

Testing later revealed a seventy-five percent displacement of the spine. After a trip to a specialist, I was told they wouldn't do anything to help me until the top half of my body fell off the bottom half. Pain killers and morphine injections brought no relief.

After a month, I decided that if I was going to fall apart, it would be while worshiping the Lord. While home alone, I turned on praise and worship music and grabbed a small red worship flag, symbolizing the blood of Jesus. Pushing through pain and tears, in song and movement I declared, **"He himself bore (my) sins in his body on the cross, so that (I) might die to sins and live for righteousness; by his wounds (I) have been healed"** (1 Pt 2:24).

Each movement, though extremely limited, was a declaration of the finished work of Jesus on the cross. Slowly the movements became more fluid as the pain gradually decreased. By aligning my heart in worship with God, God was aligning my body to His Word through worship movement. Though healing wasn't complete, I was now free to walk and move without pain, although still with limitations.

Worship movement, plus the prophetic declaration of the Word of God created the path for healing. It would take over two years and much prayer for the effects of my fall to completely dissipate, but it was through worship dance that God initiated the healing.

That was eleven years ago. Worship dance continues to be a strategic part of my spiritual warfare and intercession. With dance movement, I declare over others the freedom and breakthrough God has given me.

There hasn't been any medical intervention to restore my spine. Although I know the displacement still exists, I work and move unhindered, pain-free and with strength.

Can worship dance be prayer? Does God inspire different forms of creative movement as intercessory petition? What about painting, writing, or other forms of creativity while co-operating with the sensed movements of Heaven? Are these legitimate forms of prayer intercession through which we can take back territory for the Kingdom of God?

Personal Perspective

Candice's creative intercession flows through music and art.

"I enjoyed color when I was young and loved art in high school as I learned about famous artists, brush strokes and landscapes. For me, however, prophetic painting began after high school. I had attended a conference in Idaho where Shawn Boltz, Bobby Connor and Bob Jones were speaking. Shawn shared his desire to see the renaissance arts come to the church.

"My friends and I caught the vision and built a silkscreen, putting doodles on t-shirts. We also bought washable crayons and made murals on the walls depicting the different ways God reaches humanity. Beauty is a reflection of the glory of God, so I believe we need to value creative things.

"About a year later, God showed me an image and gave me the Scripture for intercession to go with it. I painted it and liked it so much I asked God to give me another picture. Through His silence, I knew I needed to use a blank canvas and begin painting by faith, sensing the color to start with and what brush strokes He wanted me to use. I was apprehensive because painting materials were expensive.

"One beautiful spring day, I started a prophetic painting out on the deck while listening to worship music. Halfway through the song, I knew what the picture was going to be about. The subject of the painting was intense, with bodies floating in the water. The picture was deep intercession for lost souls—a difficult word declaring that the time is coming when it will be too late to be rescued. The picture called people to turn their hearts to the Lord. I knew the painting and intercession went together.[1]

> *I could put paint on canvas and it would be a picture,*
> *but it is the approach and process that*
> *make painting intercession.*

"I would be prompted by waking up with two colors in my mind that I knew needed to be put to canvas, but I didn't want to move ahead until I knew what the Spirit was telling me to do.

"Some paintings can take two years to finish. The process requires waiting on Holy Spirit to speak while posturing my heart to be sensitive to His voice and listen. When I don't have the prompts, I stop and wait for another wave of impression from God.

"In devotion time, when I sit at the piano or with the guitar, I hang out with God through music. It is interesting how I start with me ministering to Him and He turns it around, speaking and ministering back to me. I find myself crying because He turns around my songs and sings them back to my heart.

"When God is speaking, I try to sing those things out in free-song. As I sing, He sings over me His truth, giving me faith to believe it. Free-song is a way to keep my heart right before Him, worshiping and releasing His truth."

Keegan moves powerfully in intercessory movement as well.

"I learned how to soak in God's Presence, not because I was obligated to, but because I was seeking Him. Through worship music, I focused on Him, listening to the words of the songs.

"Those times turned into worshiping and dancing alone in the sanctuary—just me and God. They became intimate times of hearing His voice and responding to Him. Sometimes after a couple of hours praising, listening and receiving, as I poured myself out in dance, His Spirit poured into me. It was an intimate soothing experience of knowing He was present with me.

> *Prayer became more proactive rather than reactive.*

"There was a gradual progression of learning what God had for me, but I struggled with just receiving from Him.

"Predominantly now when I dance, it is warring for what I feel God is wanting to do in a worship service, in me or over a circumstance. When I pick up my flags and fabric, it is to do battle against a very real enemy. I press into God through dance and fight. God has already won the war, but I do battle in dance intercession.

"It is invigorating as I become actively involved in what God is doing."

A new experience opened Charlene to prophetic intercession through music.

"When I heard the term 'prophetic intercession through instruments,' it was the first time I made the connection between prophecy, prayer and music.

"Twenty years ago, the Holy Spirit showed me that He wanted to move through music. A major shift in prayer-movement came for me through playing music prophetically. I didn't understand it at first, but all of a sudden, I began to play the piano differently. All I knew was that I was hearing things through the Spirit and somehow my hands knew how to play what I didn't know how to play. What I heard was always a note ahead; I just tried to catch up.

"We need to follow the Holy Spirit as we worship and listen. I still struggle with not coming to prayer knowing what is going to happen. Sometimes God tells me ahead of time, other times I'm waiting for direction."

Amanda^C said,

"When I was a child, my mom and grandmother sang me to sleep with worship songs. I learned to sing before I could speak. Amazing Grace was the first tune I sang before I had the words to go with it.

"My earliest childhood memories are of us being in church during worship. It was during a worship service that I accepted Jesus Christ as my Savior without anyone else leading me. I could see everyone enjoying God's Presence. I felt like I was on the outside but wanted in. I remembered my Sunday School teachers had told us about asking Jesus to come into our hearts, so that's what I did. After I accepted Christ as Savior, I was able to enjoy His Presence too.

> *For me, worship is an instant connection with God.*

"When my pastor moved away, I was devastated. I realized I had become complacent in my relationship with God. Even though I had always viewed my faith as my own, I knew that I had been relying on the faith of my pastor to carry me through.

"When my heart was broken, I pressed into God even more through worship on the piano. I didn't have anything tangible to pray, but I knew He was healing my heart as I spent time worshiping. His Presence was seeping into all the cracks in me, healing the broken places. This was the backdrop to my extended season of a lifestyle of fasting.

"Whether it is painting, dancing or praying in tongues with groanings, it is prayer. I once had the opportunity to teach the visual arts component in the Master's Commission worship class. Painting instruction was part of my lecture on prophetic art and prayer. With some paintings I've done, only later did I realize that they were prophetic intercessions on behalf of someone."

Christie said,

"The Holy Spirit has filled every place in me with comfort, strength and peace. When I approach God, I know that He is sovereign.

"He is King of all kings.
He is a Father who cares.
He is powerful.
He is majestic.

"At one point, I felt like I needed the Holy Spirit to fill me in a deep way. That need became the reason for my praise. Now I praise God for who He is, not for what He does for me. I approach Him for who He is on His own without anything coming back to me.

"Either prayer or worship comes first. You may pray to the point of praise which leads to worship, or worship may lead to prayer. For myself, I can approach God in prayer more comfortably and confidently after I've declared who He is and I've aligned my heart with Him. Then when I pray, I'm sure and believe.

"While leading worship, I pray, 'What do You want to do at

this moment? How are You ministering to people? Is there anything You want to say, Lord?' As a worship leader, I'm connecting with God so I can lead better.

"Prayer and worship are deeply connected. Sometimes we can elevate worship above prayer because people tend to worship more than pray. I don't think it was ever supposed to be that way.

"We have to get back to prayer so we can listen to God."

Amanda⁵ said,

"Through worship and dance, I learned to spend time with God. I was in a deep pit of depression and self-loathing. God reached in and pulled me out far enough for me to grab the hands of a few women with a great deal of peace in their lives. Their graceful dancing in worship inspired me. Joy and peace exuded from their whole beings as they worship danced.

"I felt such a tug on my heart to pursue that same God-connection. I prayed for God's help and then stepped out to join them in maybe one of the bravest things I had done to that time.

"I learned more about the connection between worship and listening. Soon, I became more excited to hear God's voice and heart for both His people and for me. As God spoke to my spirit, I would dance it out.

"At times, I dance without hearing or feeling anything, either due to my stubbornness, exhaustion or hardness of heart. Other times the prophetic word I'm dancing isn't for me. In those times, I have to trust that God is touching others, and I dance out of obedience.

"Worship dance has become such an intimate place for me to

express myself. I never face condemnation when I am with Holy Spirit in dance. He is always there

> teaching me new things by His grace,
>> leading me to discover my pain and stressors,
>>> showing me the depth of His Presence,
>>>> and revealing His healing power.

"I have been completely remade in these years of exploring intercession through worship dance."

Music played a strategic part in one breakthrough for Karin.

"At church, the leadership made room for a quiet time of prayer and singing to the Lord. I was standing at the front of the sanctuary when a song began to flow through me. I began to sing to God, telling Him what was going on and how I didn't know what to do.

"Another couple came to pray for me and my marriage. When I went home, it was unreal the change that had occurred and how God had turned my husband's heart. The things that matter to us, matter to God. He responds to our prayer.

"As I am praying Scripture, honestly pouring out my heart to God, I am casting my burden on Him. Alignment with the Word and prayer is integral. The more I come to know the character of God, the more I begin to read His Word with the understanding of how much He loves me. **'The people who know their God shall be strong, and carry out great exploits'** (Dn 11:32 NKJV).

"When I worship on the piano or join others in song, worship becomes an expression of great thankfulness. At other times, worship can be mournful and lamenting while waiting for freedom to come.

> *Whether praying in word or song,*
> *we declare God's restorative grace plan.*

"God always has a way of doing things that is restorative. I have seen so many results from praying through song."

Karli shared her experiences.

"God is so random that I just try to stay in tune with Him, catching whatever He is doing. Whether that means dancing around the house, prophetic acts, worshiping Him through music and song or laying on my face receiving from Him. Every day is different.

"Singing to the Lord can be a very powerful prayer. If prayer is speaking or having a conversation, then singing takes the same words putting them into a different frequency. When I sing, I sing the cry of my heart. Sometimes it's only one word; other times the words flow together freely.

"Everything is Scripture-based. Songs give adoration to God as praise or thankfulness, proclaiming His love, or declaring and decreeing Scripture over my life or a situation from the point of victory through the cross.

"I have had times when a song broke or shifted something in a moment that I had been praying about for a long time.

> *The Bible says out of the abundance of the heart, the mouth*
> *speaks.[2] Out of the abundance of the heart,*
> *the mouth also sings.*

"Movement and dance are linked to prayer when we surrender and only move based on how God directs. When I move or dance, I feel the Lord's wind and know that it is linked to Heaven. I always sense His power on it and when I don't, I stop.

"For us to see God's will done on earth, we need to catch what He is doing, whether through

> prayer and supplication,
>> sitting and waiting,
>>> worship and song,
>>>> or dance and movement.

"God is a God of mystery. When we do what He is asking us to do, He pours His anointing on it."

The psalms were written by various authors under a wide range of circumstances. Some were written as a thanksgiving to God after battles won or declarations of Lord's sovereign care in the face of great opposition.

It isn't a far stretch that God would desire us to sing His promises during struggle just as the original authors and composers did. It surprised Dawn, however, when God called her to sing His Word.

"God continues to make the importance of His Word clear to me. Since I was a small child, I have been thankful for songs which come straight from Scripture.

I know his Word is hidden in my heart in song.

"During a financially challenging time, I was feeling lost and afraid. I began praying the Scripture about God giving beauty from ashes (Is 61:1-3). God challenged me to sing it.

" 'I can't sing that!' I said.

"He said, 'Whisper it if you can't sing it.'

**'The Spirit of the Sovereign LORD is on me, because
the LORD has anointed me to proclaim good news to
the poor. He has sent me to bind up the brokenhearted,
to proclaim freedom for the captives and release from
darkness for the prisoners, to proclaim the year of the
LORD's favor, and the day of vengeance of our God,
to comfort all who mourn, and provide for those who
grieve in Zion – to bestow on them a crown of beauty instead of ashes, the oil of joy instead of mourning, and
a garment of praise instead of a spirit of despair. They
will be called oaks of righteousness, a planting of
the LORD for the display of his splendor.'**

"As I began to whisper the Word, it became life. When dreams
had become ashes, I could whisper His promises, and then
even sing them a few times. Soon, I was bawling as God deeply
ministered to my heart.

"It is always His Word, His eternal promises, that bring peace
when we are hurting and in times of despair. When we forget
that Jesus is the Prince of Peace, we try to self-soothe.

"He has taught me that in prayer I can accept moments of
calm, understanding the peace He offers. The more I grasp
and claim His Word in prayer, the more I experience the peace
available through Him no matter how fearful or unsure my
circumstances.

"Lately, Psalm 18 has become powerful and real to me. It's
beautiful!"

Jewell said,

"Prayer often feels like worship. When you worship, you are led to pray and vice versa. We come close to God both in prayer and worship with that communication carrying on even after we're done.

"Most of the songs I write are inspired by or come directly out of the words of Scripture. When I'm reading my Bible and praying, songs naturally flow.

"One time, my friend and I were entertaining at a seniors' home. We were singing a song nobody would have known, but I kept thinking that people were singing along. I looked, but nobody's mouths were moving. I was confused because I distinctly heard other voices singing in harmony with us.

"When we were finished and putting equipment back in the vehicle, my friend's husband asked, 'Did you hear somebody else singing with you tonight?'

" 'Yes,' I said, 'but I don't know where it came from. I think it might have been angels.'

"He said, 'Jewell, that's exactly what I thought. I heard it too.'

"I don't know why we heard angels singing that day, but it was beautiful. We knew Heaven was joining with us, or we were joining with Heaven.

"Quite often when I don't know what or how to pray, I tell God about it through a song. He knows the whats and the hows of my circumstances.

"The first song I wrote was a song about my redemption, how I felt God calling me and what He was calling me into."

Kimberly also finds that music and singing connects her to the rythmns of Heaven.

"Another thing I do is sing my prayers more than I speak them. Singing prayers for me is

singing random phrases,
singing in the Spirit,
singing with my understanding,
singing Scriptures,
or singing actual songs.

"It drives my husband a little crazy when we are praying together because he doesn't function like that at all.

"To me when I sing, the atmosphere changes. Singing has always been where I meet with God. Something shifts inside of me and I feel His tangible Presence more when I sing prayer than when I speak. Even when I was a teenager, I'd be in the shower (probably for too long) belting it out; I was in my God zone. Singing has always been an instant connection where I meet God, plugging into Him."

Kristina shared,

"Prayer is probably one of the most creative and unique processes. It is almost as unique or as creative as God has made each one of us. There is a creative expression on prayer. There are definitely guidelines in coming with a pure heart and there's more that I want to learn about authority, but prayer is a tapestry. Prayer expresses the creativity of the Father's heart."

Unlocking the Legacy

Can artistic expression be the prayer that unlocks legacy? Is it possible for music, dance, painting and other forms of creative expression to release the promises and intentions of God on Earth?

Heather Clark gives an emphatic, "Yes!" in her book, *Dance as The Spirit Moves.*[3]

Dance, as well as any other creative forms, may at times
break down walls, bring deliverance and freedom,
ignite passionate worship, release celebration, or
usher in healing, salvation, and victory.

When I consider aspects of artistry, nothing exceeds God's creative extravagance when He formed the Heavens and the earth. All creation invites us to bend, stretch and explore creative expression.

> **"God's splendor is a tale that is told; his testament
> is written in the stars. Space itself speaks his story
> every daythrough the marvels of the Heavens.
> His truth is on tour in the starry vault of the sky,
> showing his skill in creation's craftsmanship.
> Each day gushes out its message to the next,
> night with night whispering its knowledge to all.
> Without a sound, without a word, without a voice
> being heard, Yet all the world can see its story.
> Everywhere its gospel is clearly read
> so all may know."
> Psalm 19:1-4 TPT**

When God desired to be with His people, He gave Moses the elaborate details for each element of the tabernacle. This would be the dwelling place of the Most High God where people would worship.

> **"Then the LORD spoke to Moses, saying: 'See, I
> have called by name Bezalel . . . And I have filled
> him with the Spirit of God, in wisdom, in
> understanding, in knowledge, and in all manner
> of workmanship, to design artistic works, to work
> in gold, in silver, in bronze, in cutting jewels for
> setting, in carving wood, and to work in all manner
> of workmanship. And I, indeed I, have appointed
> with him Aholiab . . . and I have put wisdom in the**

**hearts of all the gifted artisans, that they may make
all that I have commanded you."
Exodus 31:1-6 NKJV**

God still calls, fills and anoints gifted artisans with **"wisdom, understanding, knowledge and all manner of workmanship"** to create artistic expressions of worship, releasing His glory to the world around us.

Every God-anointed creative movement
with hammer or brush,
with clay or with cloth,
in gold or silver,
in word or movement,
is a representation, though limited, of our Creator.

*"(We are) called to be part of raising up a generation
of worshipers who operate in the healing anointing and
release God's Presence through all kinds of creative ways."* [4]

The Bible affirms dance, both individually and corporately, as a significant and powerful expression of worship, celebrating God's Presence and victory over the enemy. Over twenty-five years ago, I stood awestruck as I watched public worship dance for the first time. In praying intercession I had danced before God in the privacy of my own home many times, but to see it as a public form of worship stirred something deep within me to pursue worship in this new-old way.

The first biblical account of dance and worship involved an eighty-five-year-old woman and over a million people.

**"Then Miriam the prophet, Aaron's sister, took
a timbrel in her hand, and all the women followed
her, with timbrels and dancing. Miriam sang to
them: 'Sing to the LORD; for he is highly exalted.
Both horse and driver he has hurled into the sea.' "
Exodus 15:20,21**

This brother-sister dual of Moses and Miriam led the greatest worship service ever conducted. There on the banks of the Red Sea, as they watched their mortal enemy floating dead on the waves, four hun-

dred and thirty years of oppression was drowned forever (Ex 12:40).
From slavery to freedom,
oppression to deliverance,
poverty to abundance,
now captives no more,
they sang and danced.

When I remember what God has done in my own life, separating
my past from my present, I can't help but break into similar worship.
He has
released me from an inescapable pit,
shattered the chains of addictions,
softened and healed my
hardened and broken heart,
renewed my mind once clouded by depression
and filled me with a passion to live sold-out for Him.
For me, it's time to dance!

> **"Then young women will dance and be glad,**
> **young men and old as well. I will turn their**
> **mourning into gladness; I will give them com-**
> **fort and joy instead of sorrow."**
> **Jeremiah 31:13**

Sometimes dance expresses joyous gratitude toward God. At
other times, God himself inspires and motivates believers to dance.
The first verse in the Bible describes the Holy Spirit actively descend-
ing over the formless void establishing God's rhythm and movement.

> **"In the beginning, God created the Heaven and the**
> **earth. Now the earth was formless**
> **and empty, darkness was over the**
> **surface of the deep and the Spirit of God**
> **was hovering over the waters."**
> **Genesis 1:1-2**

Hovering resembles an eagle fluttering over her young, shaking and
trembling, vibrating and moving. By divine strategy and in preparation for creation, Holy Spirit actively moved, fluttered and shook. After
the Holy Spirit "danced," then God spoke the elements into existence.

Creativity and movement have been linked together by God Himself.

David perhaps best illustrates another purpose for dance. He longed for the Ark of God's Presence to return to Jerusalem. His first attempt failed with Uzzah losing his life, but David didn't give up.

> **"Wearing a linen ephod, David was dancing
> before the LORD with all his might, while he and
> all Israel were bringing up the ark of the LORD
> with shouts and the sound of trumpets."**
> **2 Samuel 6:14-15**

I'm reminded how David danced before the Presence of God came. Unrestrained, undignified, no-holds-barred dancing before God! Dressed as a priest, the king led. As a result, all Israel followed.

Extravagant, vulnerable worship is risky. For those desiring to usher in the Presence of God, creative artistry can be costly. Some, like David's wife, will misunderstand such devotion, rejecting what God calls pure and beautiful (2 Sm 6:16). God honors and protects those who without reservation give Him all their worship as David did.

> **"...I will celebrate before the LORD. I will become
> even more undignified than this, and I will be
> humiliated in my own eyes."**
> **2 Samuel 6:21-22**

Worship includes quiet, solitary encounters with God, but not always. Every creative expression of adoration to the Lord also paints a demonstration of worship. How does God respond?

> **"The LORD your God is with you, the Mighty War-
> rior who saves. He will take great delight in you;
> in his love he will no longer rebuke you, but will
> rejoice over you with singing."**
> **Zephaniah 3:17**

God, the Mighty Warrior, rises with great delight to our worship efforts, twirling and spinning *"over (us) with singing."* Am I exaggerating? Not at all! The word "rejoice" means to be "bright, cheerful, and having great joy, twirling and spinning."[4] When God rises in collaboration with our frail but expressive worship, dancing breaks forth on Earth and in Heaven. Wow!

Prayer-filled creative artistry effectively fights spiritual battles. They are strategic forms of warfare against our enemy. One only has to look at 2 Chronicles 20 as proof. King Jehoshaphat sent his worshipers ahead of the army to face a fierce military coalition. They arrived at the battle line prepared for combat but discovered the enemy had annihilated themselves. Worship declares victory in battle, refusing to give the enemy our time or attention.

During one particular service, all the fathers were invited to the altar to take a stand in prayer and petition for their families. Suddenly, it was as if I was pushed out of my comfortable pew into the aisle to dance in warfare for broken families and prodigals. Within a week, our own prodigal returned home. Was it a coincidence? Hardly! The combination of prayer, warfare and dance accomplished what years of prayer alone seemed powerless to do.

Creativity used as an expression of worship to God is a mighty, sometimes non-verbal, declaration of love and adoration to the King of kings and Lord of lords, ushering in His Presence.

> *"Prayer is an act of humility because the person who prays acknowledges the need for Heaven's help and fellowship with the Creator."* [5]

Taking Territory

"Lord, 'since the creation of the world, (Your) invisible qualities—(Your) eternal power and divine nature—have been clearly seen, being understood from what has been made' (Rom 1:20).

"God, enable us to perpetuate creative expressions that reflect Your goodness and greatness. In so doing, may we touch Your heart and move Your hand.

"Oh Lord, help us to see and know You in new ways through creative expression re-presenting You here and now to others. I ask You to give us greater freedom in artistic expression through music, drama, videography, dance, and artistry of all kinds. Call, fill and anoint Your artisans with skill. May a fresh and powerful worship prayer movement arise, catching Heaven's currents and releasing them to earth through creative acts—rejuvenating, re-establishing, re-presenting Your heart to others.

"We ask for bodies to be healed,
> victories to be won,
>> salvations to birth,
>>> walls of division to crumble,
>> deliverance to be brought, and
> awe and celebration of Your goodness
to explode around us,

through the release of artistry and movement. Do it again, Lord! We refuse to confine creativity to days gone by or yield it to enemy purposes. We hunger to witness for ourselves the liberty and power of creative movements, unlocking legacy.

"Inspire and motivate us to release Your Word and will into the earth in creative ways. We lay down preconceived notions of what prayer is and is not. May all our creative acts be offerings of prayer and worship before Your throne.

"Guard our hearts against critical judgments of the creative expressions You are releasing now in prayer. Where the river of Holy Spirit initiative flows, there is life (Ez 47:9). May the river of creative movement in prayer birth Kingdom life throughout the nations.

"Release in people of all ages a creative prayer movement that will take back territory from the enemy, securing it for You. Anoint artistry in this season so that when people hear and see creative expressions they would be transformed by the embrace of Heaven.

"Come, Lord! Raise up again sons and daughters like Bezalel, **'filled . . . with the Spirit of God, with wisdom, with understanding, with knowledge and with all kinds of skills—to make artistic designs . . . to engage in all kinds of crafts,'** creating sanctuaries of worship, prayer and adoration unto You (Ex 31:1-6). Do it again!

"May women pick up the timbrels of warfare and men raise their feet in worship dance, rejoicing as You
> part the seas of obstruction,
>> drown the enemy who enslaves,

fight for the defenseless,
                and bring your salvation (Ex 15).
"Open our eyes in prayer to see and our ears to hear, then give us the boldness to cooperate with Heaven. Make us strong and courageous! Today we take back the territory the enemy has held in trust for us. We turn this key with your authority unlocking legacy which will affect generations to come.

Amen."

*"I was waiting for a moment—an encounter.
Out of worship the encounters, the moments, come."
– Joy-Lyn*

***

*"God has made clear to me the importance of learning and spending time in His Word. I always feel like His Word is hidden in my heart in song."
– Dawn*

***

*"Expressing God's heart through movement is the most natural way of feeling God's Presence. There is a whole other level in the prophetic, releasing God's heart through movement—passionately feeling His heart and catching it in dance."
– Amanda* S.

***

Notes:

1. Candice Snyder, "Candisart: The Original Artwork of Candice Snyder," https://www.candisart.com/

2. Luke 6:45

3. Heather Clark, *Dance as the Spirit Moves: A Practical Guide to Worship and Dance* (Shippensburg, Destiny Image Publishers Inc., 2009), 132-135.

4. James Strong, S.T.D., LL.D., *Strong's Exhaustive Concordance of the Bible* (Peabody, Hendrickson Publishers, 1990), s.v. "rejoice", 1523.

5. Bill Johnson and Kris Vallotton, *The Supernatural Ways of Royalty: Discovering Your Rights and Privileges of Being a Son or Daughter of God* (Shippensburg: Destiny Image Publishers, 2006), 113.

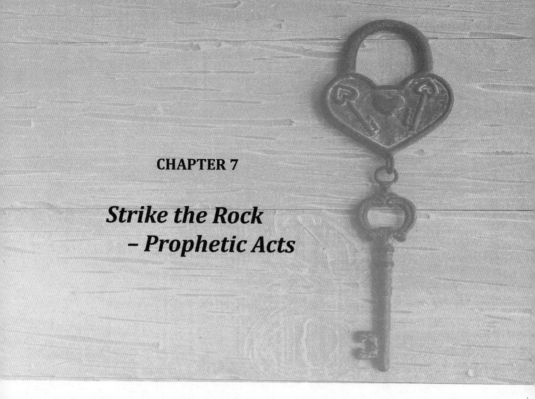

CHAPTER 7

Strike the Rock – Prophetic Acts

> *"Prayer is masterminding with the Most High God."*
> *– Charlene* S

The little group of intercessors gathered, sensing a need to pray for their city and local churches. Each came with an expectation, and perhaps even a preconceived agenda, of what would be accomplished through prayer. However, God had a much different design and purpose in mind.

As they met together for the first time, a holy hush settled distinctly within their ranks, sealing their lips and opening their hearts to the unexpected. No one could utter a word. The air felt heavy with the sovereign Presence of God. Gently, the Spirit moved among them as holy awe filled the little room where they met.

The next week was a repeat; the following week was more of the same. Week after week, meeting after meeting, God unraveled all preconceived patterns of what prayer looks, sounds and feels like.

When God finally released them to speak, it was only through Scriptures sung while accompanied by instruments played in the Spirit.

For each of those attending, it was an awkward time of relearning and submitting to the whispered direction from God. In faith, these seasoned prayer warriors and intercessors yielded, allowing God to lead as they followed this uncharted territory of prayer initiative.

After several months of gathering together, they felt the Holy Spirit nudging them to take prayer for their city into the streets. They sensed that they were to walk silently, claiming their city with the soles of their feet as well as the prayers of their lips. **"Every place that the sole of your foot will tread upon I have given you . . ."** (Jo 1:3 KJV).

First, one person led; then another moved to the forefront; each taking a turn as they went through the streets. In a silent procession, they walked past schools, businesses and recreation centers. Stopping briefly at sites known for occult activity and slowing at places where people had been exposed to ungodly influences, they reclaimed their city for God.

For most of the afternoon, they prayed without uttering a word as they walked. Sometimes the heavy burden for their city brought them to tears, other times to righteous anger. At certain places, God seemed to stop the band of praying intercessors to listen more intently and pray more earnestly.

As this secret squad of warriors marched, they inconspicuously carried unfurled worship flags as silent declarations of God's sovereignty and authority over their city. With paper and pencil, they quietly recorded the strategies God revealed to each of them through the Spirit at various locations.

Some weeks later, they sensed an urgency to establish protection over every natural entrance to their city. As they prayed together before embarking on their mission, they felt a mixture of apprehension and anticipation. Their faith was stretched by the new prayer territory into which they were moving.

This time, they went by night. They drove together through the city, worshiping God and calling upon Him to intervene over their community and all the people in it. With flashlights, shovels and Bibles, they stood vigil at every place where destructive intruders might gain access to their city. At the points of entrance into their community, both by air and land, they buried Bibles and declared Scriptures. They confessed the sins of past generations, called for unity between the churches and welcomed a move of the Holy Spirit. They agreed in prayer that their city and territory belonged to God, and would be a welcome and safe place for people of all ages and nationalities. They stationed themselves in prayer, creating a boundary of protection around their community and planting the Word of God into the fertile soil of faith.

Each of these God-inspired prophetic acts required new levels of trusting the Holy Spirit's direction. Each one accomplished largely unseen things in the Heavenly realm, as they played

> instruments and sang Scripture,
>> walked their community with unfurled flags,
>>> drove the streets while worshiping God,
>>>> and buried the unchanging truth
>>>>> around the perimeter of their city.

What resulted from these prophetic prayer initiatives? Only Heaven will tell the full impact. Significant and tangible changes were witnessed, however. A major production and distribution center for drugs was uncovered by law enforcement and charges were laid. Significant shifts in the governing authority of the community occurred. Pastoral changes in churches allowed for greater unity locally and regionally.

Perhaps the greatest result was in the prayer lives of each of these prophetic warriors themselves. They gained greater confidence in their ability to hear, respond, and cooperate with the initiatives of Heaven to see changes on Earth. Faith increased and with it, humility and boldness.

Personal Perspectives

God directed Charlene to lay bricks and shoot arrows.

"One of the men in our prayer group saw in the Spirit five bricks with specific words written on them. He explained that

while looking down from the top, they appeared uncon-
nected—three across and two in the spaces. However, when he
looked at them straight on, they formed a wall. How they
appeared depended on perspective.

"We drew the bricks on paper, placing them on the floor the
way he had seen them. Then we began to pray how the Holy
Spirit showed him.

"That was in the spring. In January that same year, we had a
time of prayer and fasting. In the prayer room one night during
worship, even though I wasn't sure why, I reached back into my
quiver and started pulling arrows out. I kept shooting arrows.
Then I thought, 'Okay that's good enough.'

"God urged, 'Do another one!'

"It was a prophetic act. I didn't understand what it was for, I
just knew that was what God wanted us to do. As we kept praying, I felt like I was to stand and face the place of government
in our community. I took an arrow out of my quiver and shot
it into five areas of government. In the natural it was utterly
irrational, but we did it. Then we thanked God.

"We took one week where we just listened. The next week, we
acted on what we had heard and again did what we thought the
Holy Spirit was leading us to do. Then my husband and I left
for a conference.

"While we were gone, one thing triggered another that was
very public. God completely undid the current government,
removing people who needed to be removed. Through
elections, God put in a new government.

"God knew what was happening and knew what needed to
change. He gave us authority in prayer and we acted on it. The
Lord had us address those things and cut off their supply,
commanding them to be broken.

"Within a few months, I read Dean Briggs' book *Ekklesia Rising* and Rebecca Greenwood's book *Glory Warfare*. The books talk about taking authority. They remind us that the church is not a building, not even a group of people, but a governing body to bring what Heaven is decreeing down on Earth. As I read, I realized that was what we had done.

"We were learning to listen prophetically, asking God for when and how He wanted things accomplished.

> *I believe that if there is a governing body of believers in every community, our nation will change.*

"I don't have authority over my nation or my province, but I have authority over my community. There have to be people in each community who know that God is calling us to stand in authority."

Heather shared,

"What if what I once thought was effective isn't? What if what I don't like is exactly what He wants me to do?

"Recently during a worship service, I felt strongly that I was supposed to begin stomping my feet loudly. No one else was stomping. I didn't know that the worship leader was praying in the Spirit for an earthquake to bring a breakthrough for our families. For me, stomping my feet on the ground was an act of faith and obedience.

"Perhaps this simple act was more effective in the Kingdom than anything else I could have said or done. It twists my mind! Shortly after, I experienced a surprising turn of events when my son called planning to visit."

Patrick briefly said,

"I had heard testimony about Kris Vallotton seeing swords in people; with that testimony, I was able to also claim the ability to see things in the spirit. There have been a few times I have had the impression of swords in someone. After either I pulled it out or had them pull it out themselves, healings followed."

Merodee began moving in prophetic action as a child, kicking the enemy out the door.

"Mom had an adult Christian book about a young girl who died of leukemia. When I read the book, I felt the invitation to be afraid of leukemia. It was really an invitation to accept death. I knew there was a battle and whatever I gave agreement to would dominate my life. If I gave into death, I would die; if I contended for life, I would live.

"I was very sick and lost a lot of weight. For almost two years, I was in a battle of whether I would give my agreement to death or life. Since I was a child, I didn't think the same way adults do. I was anxious and missed a lot of time at school.

"One day while sick at home, I watched a Christian television program in which they talked about contending and abiding. I knew it was a message for me. 'There is someone watching today. The enemy is tormenting you and you need to resist him by physically enacting kicking him out of the house.' The person on the program led us in prayer. I immediately opened the door and said, 'In Jesus' Name, go!'

"I don't think the change was immediate, but it was a turning point. Shortly after, Mom had a word of knowledge to take me to a specific doctor. Even though a referral normally would have been needed, she managed to book an appointment for me anyway. He prescribed medication and from then on I was good."

Pray, pray and pray again. I don't usually receive words of knowledge accurately, but I continue to seek God for them and step out in faith.

"Recently, I had a word of knowledge that someone was feeling tightness around the right shoulder blade. A woman came forward explaining that she constantly experiences pain and tightness in that area. She believed it resulted from a fall and head injury many years prior.

"I prayed over her head, spine and shoulder, the muscles and tendons associated with that area and any trauma experienced. There wasn't any change in her condition when I asked her to test it out.

"We prayed again and this time she felt the pain shift. I've learned that when pain shifts there is usually a spiritual connection to the physical pain.

"We began to pray a third time and she stopped me. She saw in her mind a cord wound around her spine. Since she saw the cord, I asked her to unwind it from her backbone. She reached back over her shoulder creating an unwinding motion with her hand. Then I asked her to throw away the cord and declare freedom from hindrance over her body.

"When she did, she instantly felt a distinct release. Although there was still stiffness in that area of her back, the pain was completely gone and she knew she had experienced significant healing. Unwinding the cord in her spine was the key God showed her to receive healing."

A major shift occurred in Jan's life after a shout.

"I jumped up and down yelling. I knew that yelling was the answer, even though I didn't know what the question was.

"My heart longed to join in with other churches involved with prophetic intercession, so I asked my lead pastor for his blessing. God heard my request and answered.

"I was invited as a prayer leader to a conference in another province even though I wasn't leading anything in prayer at that time. My pastor said, 'Yes! You're a prayer leader.' He prayed for me and released me to go.

"Even though pastors were saying I should take leadership, I had believed that since I was a divorced woman, it couldn't be me. When I went to those I prayed with all the time, they said, 'What are you arguing for? Of course, you're supposed to lead.' They encouraged me to keep seeking God.

"I'm prophetic and want things in black and white. I said, 'Okay, Lord, I will do it if You want me to. The direction has to come from You, not me.'

"One night, I was on my way to a prayer meeting, when God stopped me halfway down the hall with, 'I want to talk to you.'

"I was annoyed. 'I'm on my way to prayer. I'm going to be late.'

I heard Him laugh, 'No, I want to talk to you now.'

"I went into a little room we would sometimes use for prayer during a service. Sitting down, I opened my book and said, 'Okay, I'm going to write whatever You say.'

"He started to give me the template for leading prophetic intercession and said, 'You are going to do it; you're the leader.'

"I sent the template to the pastor who invited me to the prayer leaders' conference with Mike Bickle. When he blessed me over the phone, I felt something fall on me, which I believe I still wear to this day. He leads a house of prayer in that area and we continue to be in contact with each other."

> *Somehow jumping up and down and yelling was the propelling of this new area of ministry.*

Unlocking the Legacy

Under the leading of the Holy Spirit, prophetic acts are actions intentionally employed to proclaim God's message. The action, sometimes with the aid of objects, serves to present God's message more clearly. These actions are done in the natural through God's direction, declaring what He is doing or intends to do. This uniting of God-anointed action with His message constitutes a prophetic act, which forges a breakthrough in the spiritual realm.

The visual aspect of prophetic acts makes God's message unmistakably clear. Ezekiel and Jeremiah both performed several prophetic acts in the Bible. However, God-inspired actions were used by individuals from many different professions, not just prophets. Prophetic actions served many purposes.

- Elijah threw his cloak over Elisha as a **call to ministry** (I Kgs 19:19).

> **"So Elijah went from there and found Elisha son of Shaphat. He was plowing with twelve yoke of oxen . . . Elijah went up to him and threw his cloak around him."**

- Agabus tied the hands of Paul **foretelling** of imprisonment (Acts 21:10-12).

> **". . . a prophet named Agabus . . . took Paul's belt, tied his own hands and feet with it and said, "The**

> Holy Spirit says, 'In this way the Jewish leaders in
> Jerusalem will bind the owner of this belt and will
> hand him over to the Gentiles.' "

- Jeremiah bought a belt, traveled four hundred miles to bury
it, and then returned home. God later sent him back to dig
it up again, only to discover it had been ruined. It became
a sign **to warn** Israel that God was going to ruin the nation
because of her pride (Jer 13:1-7).

> "... buy a linen belt and put it around your waist ..
> . Take the belt you bought and are wearing around
> your waist, and go now to Perath and hide it there
> in a crevice in the rocks ... go now to Perath and
> get the belt I told you to hide there ... In the same
> way, I will ruin the pride of Judah and the
> great pride of Jerusalem."

- Jesus put mud in the blind man's eyes and commanded him
to wash as a prophetic act of **healing** (Jn 9:1-11).

> " ... Night is coming, when no one can work.
> While I am in the world, I am the light of the
> world. After saying this, he spit on the ground,
> made some mud with the saliva, and put it on the
> man's eyes. 'Go,' he told him, 'wash in the Pool of
> Siloam' ... so the man went and washed,
> and came home seeing."

- Striking arrows on the ground pronounced **victory** (2 Kgs
13:18).

> "Then he said, 'Take the arrows,' and the king
> took them. Elisha told him, 'Strike the ground.' He
> struck it three times and stopped. The man of God
> was angry with him and said, 'You should have
> struck the ground five or six times; then you would
> have defeated Aram and completely destroyed it.
> But now you will defeat it only three times."

- Throwing salt in water declared **life** and **productivity** over a dead and barren land (2 Kgs 2:19-22).

> " . . . the water is bad and the land is unproductive.
> 'Bring me a new bowl,' he said, 'and put salt in it.' .
> . . Then he went out to the spring and threw the salt
> into it, saying, 'This is what the LORD says: 'I have
> healed this water. Never again will it cause
> death or make the land unproductive.' "

- Wiping the dust off of feet decreed **judgment** (Mt 10:14-15).

> "If anyone will not welcome you or listen to your
> words, leave that home or town and shake the dust
> off your feet. Truly I tell you, it will be more bear-
> able for Sodom and Gomorrah on the day
> of judgment than for that town."

- Binding two sticks **declared promise** and imparted **encour-agement** (Ez 37:15-23).

> ". . . take a stick of wood and write on it, 'Belong-
> ing to Judah and the Israelites associated with
> him.' Then take another stick of wood, and write
> on it, 'Belonging to Joseph . . . and all the Israelites
> associated with him.' Join them together into one
> stick so that they will become one in your hand . . .
> I will gather them from all around and bring them
> back into their own land. I will make
> them one nation in the land . . ."

This list is not complete by any stretch of the imagination. Prophetic actions were as diverse as the messages God spoke to His people. Some were costly and difficult, even lasting an entire lifetime like Hosea marrying a prostitute. Others were as quick and easy as Nehemiah shaking out the folds of his robe (Neh 5:13).

Prophetic acts aren't reserved for the strange prophets and radical followers, however. The practices of communion (1 Cor 11:23-26) and baptism (Rom 6:1-7) are an acknowledgment of what God has already done as well as a prophetic act of what is yet to come.

Genuine prophetic actions are birthed through prayer and waiting on the Lord. They flow from humility of heart, boldness of spirit and passion for God. A person must have a sensitivity to the Holy Spirit to accurately discern whether the prophetic words and associated actions come from their own volition or under His leading.

"For prophecy never had its origin in the human will,
but prophets, though human, spoke from God as
they were carried along by the Holy Spirit."
2 Peter 1:21

Jeremiah wore a yoke to symbolize how Israel would be taken into captivity. Hananiah, a false prophet, broke the yoke to declare that their enemy would be defeated in two years. Both were recognized as prophets; one had discernment; one did not (Jer 28).

Prophetic actions combined with the declaration of God's Word can unlock legacy through expressing God's divine will and releasing His power and authority into circumstances and over territories.

So whether God directs us to bury His Word by a city gate,
stomp our feet during a worship service,
march or dance around a legislative building,
shout at an impenetrable wall,
throw water on parched soil,
or whatever other instruction is given, decree and declare His inspired word through objects and actions. Even though we may not fully understand God's purposes, let's take the risk, stepping out in faith and declare His word over people and situations.

"Although prophetic actions are at times spontaneous
and unintentional, they remain highly potent." [1]

Sometimes the word will come first in prayer and the action flows from it. At other times, the action will come first and God's word will follow. God alone knows what legacy waits to be unlocked through simple acts of obedience. Will it be healing, restoration, deliverance or the embarking on a ministry? One thing is for sure, prophetic acts have divine purpose and intention.

Taking Territory

"Lord Jesus, so often I have come to You with my needs and agenda. Today, I wait before You simply asking to know what is on Your heart. What are You desiring to change in me or around me? What is happening in my community or nation that Your heart yearns to redirect, restore, resolve or revive?

"I thank You, that You are increasing prophetic voice and action. Your intercessors are moving and speaking with Your authority and power. Spiritual momentum is beginning to intensify locally, nationally and globally in cooperation with Your heart and Spirit.

"Oh God! May we boldly put our hands upon Your hand and **'open the . . . window'** of prayer and shoot! May we **'shoot . . . the Lord's arrow of victory, the arrow of victory'** over our very real enemy **'completely destroying'** him (2Kgs 13:15-17).

"Set us on fire, Lord, with a passion for You. Ignite us to courageously take prayer out of the seclusion of our homes and into the streets of our cities. Give us ears to hear, eyes to see and faith to cooperate with Heaven to see many called in new ministry positions,

to hear Your voice of warning or judgment before it's too late,

to bring healing to individuals and nations,

to release Your promise and blessing,

to revive the dead and unproductive areas,

to declare victory during battles,

and to inspire courage and hope.

"Father, draw us into the place of humility before Your throne. Cause us to rest and wait until we hear You clearly for each prayer initiative. **'Is not (Your) word like fire . . . and like a hammer that breaks a rock in pieces'** (Jer 23:29)?

"Deliver us from traditional paradigms of what we once thought prayer should look or sound like. Break the old mold! We are hungry to hear Your voice and respond in prayer under divine inspiration. We are willing to become messy, indignant and uncomfortable for the sake of Your Kingdom advancement and for the glory of Your name.

"May we, like the prophets of old, take common objects in our hands and use them to succinctly declare Your message to those around us. Though it may seem foolish to our natural minds, we trust

127

You with our obedience. Your thoughts are not our thoughts, neither are Your ways our ways. As the Heavens are higher than the earth, so are Your ways and Your thoughts higher than our thoughts (Is 55:8-9).

"Give us humility of heart, discernment of spirit, and sensitivity to Your Presence as we learn to combine prayer and prophetic action, unlocking the legacy and bringing breakthroughs for my family, city and nation.

Amen."

> *"It's unnerving not understanding what God is doing.*
> *Yet, it is exciting to know that I am partnering with Him.*
> *Everything we are doing, we are doing it together."*
> *— Mark*

***

> *"New ceilings require new levels of prayer."*
> *— Merodee*

***

> *"We need to follow the Holy Spirit.*
> *We are going to pray and we are going to listen."*
> *— Charlene*

***

Notes
1. Charles A. Metteer, Ph.D., "Revival Fire: A Biblical Basis for Contemporary Prophetic Actions," *The World for Jesus Ministries*, July 28, 2008, https://worldforjesus.org/article/revival-fire-a-biblical-basis-for-contemporary-prophetic-actions/.

CHAPTER 8

Intimacy & Reward
– When You Fast

> *"Fasting quiets my mind to get answers."*
> *– Christie*

The crisp morning air matched the excitement in my spirit as I entered the camp tabernacle for the morning class. The gaping doors at the rear of the building were opened wide allowing the sun's rays to chase away the lingering chill. The sounds of laughing children and robins courting merged happily, filling the air with playful melody.

Gradually, the chitter-chatter of the small crowd gathering within the confines of the tabernacle settled. Their shared joy in being together and the anticipation of going deeper in their faith was indisputable. They sincerely wanted to be with and learn more about God.

In an attempt to interrupt their jabbering and begin the morning session, the speaker stepped up to the microphone and began, "What is the purpose of fasting?"

Almost scoffingly someone quickly interjected, "Fasting? Oh, that's for desperate situations and radical believers."

"Anyone else?" the teacher urged as he sat on the edge of the wooden platform waiting for further response.

An elderly woman slowly stood to her feet. Carefully choosing her words, she spoke softly, "Years ago, my husband was ready to leave me; I was more than ready to see him go. God led me to fast for three days. During that short fast, He changed everything, beginning with my own heart and attitudes. Forty years later, we are still together. Happily, I might add. God saw our tears and heard our cry. He saved our family from the brink of disaster."

Her words caused everyone to more thoughtfully consider the question.

"My mom fasted lots," a man whose age was as round as his middle offered. "Maybe why she never spoke hateful of others. She knew she needed Him as much as anyone." He pointed skyward to dispel any doubts as to his meaning.

A young mother in the back row spoke apprehensively as she rocked and cradled her fussing baby. "I think I fast because I need God . . . or more of God . . . or I mean . . . somehow fasting brings me closer to Him." Her words reached for answers as elusive and flighty as the swallows darting in and out of the open door.

The speaker resumed his place behind the microphone, beginning the morning lesson. I was lost in thought and introspection. Why do *I* fast? Why *do* I fast so often? And, quite frankly, why do I feel more than a little uncomfortable admitting, even to this group of God-seekers, how often that is.

Admittedly, I felt driven to fast, attempting to somehow twist God's seemingly reluctant arm to do things my way, to observe my desperate plight, and to come quickly to my aid. Consistently, however, through the fasting, the urgency for other things waned and the need for God's closeness prevailed. Fasting usually began focused on some current crisis but ended with only Him in view.

The speaker's words seemed to grow distant as I thought of Matthew's words, **'The time will come when the bridegroom will be taken from them; then they will fast"** (Mt 9:15). Perhaps for the first time, I saw the connection. When the world presses in and my Bridegroom seems distant, I fast to remember how close He is. When the enemy boasts of his exploits, I fast to remember the greatness and sovereignty of my Awesome God. Fasting reminds me that although the war may not be over, the victory has already been won.

Sometimes the call to remember took a day, sometimes three, maybe ten. But every fast to date had drawn me into intimacy, into sweet fellowship, with the Author and Finisher of my faith (Heb 12:2).

And with the fast, I was changed—becoming
a little more tender toward others,
a little more aware of my own spiritual need,
a little more sensitive to God's call to come closer,
a little more responsive to the Spirit's directive,
a little more yielded and humble to His will,
a little more like Him and less like me
—the old me, the ragged me, the harsh and broken me.

I realized that fasting is essential for the health of my soul: fasting from busyness and noise, fasting from food and comfort, fasting from people and pleasure, fasting from the things that pacify and numb me into indifference.

Too soon, a gaggle of children exploded into the sanctuary bringing an awkward end to the class, but not to my thoughts.

What *is* my purpose for fasting?
Fasting fuels my longing for God.
Fasting re-establishes Him as Lord in my life.
Fasting awakes concern for others.
Fasting realigns my heart with His.

"When you fast," I heard the Spirit whisper, **"don't look like those who pretend to be spiritual . . . realize that the Father in the secret place is the One who is watching all that you do . . . and will continue to reward you openly"** (Mt 6:16).

I smiled as I walked out into the warmth of the noonday sun. Turning from the crowd which was heading toward the dining hall, I stolled down the earthen path to sit alone by the meandering creek. "When you fast," His words invited me again, "there is divine purpose and open reward." The maple bough's leaned low overhead concealing our meeting between the Father and His daughter, alone together. God's peace settled not upon but rather in me.

"Yes, Daddy," my heart whispered back, "I welcome Your invitation to set aside other things and be with You. The only reward I desire is You and Your Presence."

Personal Perspectives

Fasting had a great influence on Keegan's prayer life.

"Even though I was trying to do ministry, I was constantly irritated with others. God showed me that I could choose to stay miserable, depressed and angry. I knew I needed to come back to my relationship with God to get healed or I would keep spiraling downward.

"About that time, a friend reached out to me, encouraging me to attend Bible school. It was at Bible school that I started going through a lot of cleansing and healing of my heart. I prayed and fasted often as I laid the groundwork that lined up with God's calling on my life. Yes, there was a lot of prayer and fasting as I sought God and pressed into Him.

"Even during longer fasts, I didn't feel slowed down or negatively impacted by it. I had an almost audible knowing what God was saying and what He was asking me to do.

> *Fasting is about a deepening of our relationship with God.*

"Fasting spring-boarded me into a renewed relationship with Him. I did a Nazarite Vow for two years and added a sugar fast too. No matter what I craved, I said, 'Man does not live by this, that, or the next thing.' After a couple of years, I felt a much deeper connection with God.

"Even now when I fast, I sense an extra boost from the signals of Heaven regarding what God is wanting to say and do. When God calls you to fast, there's a special grace over it because He's drawing you closer to Himself."

Nicole's fast from social media taught her more than she bargained for.

"I recently did a forty-day media fast. For other people, it might not have been significant, but for me it was. I quit everything considered social media including movies, television and podcasts. It was so good! Even though I want to live my whole life that way now, I know that's not reasonable. I'm trying to steward what I've learned.

"My brother-in-law prayed, 'God let every passion of Nicole's heart be submitted to You.' Instantly, in a vision, I saw myself lying on my bed with my head toward the end of the bed. Several books I was reading were spread out on the bed. Everything in my bedroom looked normal except my bedspread was different. I heard God invite me to do a forty-day media fast.

"I felt led to clean my house from top to bottom at the same time as the fast. Every single place I could clean, I cleaned. I donated most of my clothes and tossed out half my stuff. I felt the significance of this house cleaning even in the areas that don't often get looked at. In those forty days, everything was getting swept out.

> *The house cleaning mirrored the deep cleaning going on inside me.*

"Since my bed has a broken leg and scratches the floor when moved, it doesn't get moved often. During the cleaning though, I moved my bed to the other side of the room. There were about fifteen water bottles under where it had been.

"During the fasting and cleaning, I thought, 'I'm going to rearrange the furniture in my bedroom.'

"I heard Holy Spirit emphatically say, 'NO!'

"I said, 'Excuse me! This is my bedroom.'

"I heard it so strong again, 'NO!'

"Still, I argued, 'Why not?'

"Again, I could hear Him say, 'NO!'

" 'Even if it doesn't work, at least I will have learned for my-self why not.' I started rearranging my bedroom with the full knowledge that I had been told, 'No.' It probably only took ten minutes to move everything around. When I went to put the last piece of furniture into place, I remembered, 'Oh right!'

"I forgot about the heater that comes out from the wall. I couldn't put my desk there. Then I realized that nothing about the new arrangement worked. There wasn't any piece of furniture that could go in that spot and that was why I had my furniture the way it previously was.

"I conceded, 'Alright, I get it. At least now I know.'

"Then I started to put all the furniture back. Every piece felt like it weighed a thousand pounds. It took me an hour and a half to put everything back the way it was. In the end, I even scratched the floor with the bed. When I finally finished, I collapsed on the bed exhausted because it took so long.

"God said to me, 'In this next season, you're going to find freedom like you haven't had before. Freedom to do things you didn't think were ever possible for you. The temptation to rearrange your life will be so strong, but stay obedient to the vision I've given you.' "

Christie shared her fasting experience.

"When I have anxiety or I'm trying to figure things out, I need to fast. Fasting removes me from the process and allows God to speak.

"Fasting quiets my mind to get answers. One time, I fasted, prayed, and walked away with peace but I said, 'I don't think I know the answer.' I knew God's answer even though for a long time I denied it.

> *When we ask God specific questions,*
> *we get specific answers.*

"When I fast, I quiet myself and stop talking. For me, the big thing is settling myself to listen. Whatever I hear from God, I write down. Often when I'm fasting and writing things down, there will be a Bible verse I never really noticed before that begins to speak to me powerfully. At that moment, God gives what we need to keep going and have peace of mind knowing He heard us.

"Some things are only answered by prayer and fasting. Fasting is something we need to do more than just when we need something big. We always need to hear from God.

"I fast intermittently, trying to find balance. Is it okay to fast even when you aren't being intentional at that moment? Is God still going to be honored in it? I don't want to fast just for the sake of fasting.

"I've seen breakthroughs through fasting for myself. Recently, I spent three days without any distractions from technology and social media. I woke up early, wrote, spent time with the Lord and was intentional in the process. I heard Him through it.

"Right now, I'm in school but feel unsettled in the application process. Am I moving? Am I staying? I want to know. While praying about it, I felt God say, 'Wait. Just wait. It's okay.' God gave me peace through the process, knowing

His plan will be fulfilled.

"I have seen other people fast longer and get set free from big areas in their lives. At other times the clarity doesn't come during the fast but afterward. You know that it's an answer to prayer and fasting. Often answers come in ways you didn't even think possible."

Kate said,

"A major turning point that drew me deeper into prayer happened when my health issues became serious. Because I couldn't be physically active, I took advantage of the time and spent it with the Lord in prayer. It became a season of pressing into the Lord and reading the Word.

"Because I didn't have a lot of other demands on my life, I could spend more time in prayer and fasting. That disciplined season of fasting carried on for about ten years.

"Fasting births greater obedience to the Lord in what He wants to accomplish. To a huge degree, a person becomes less aware of the flesh and more in tune with Holy Spirit. The focus during fasting is on the Lord, intently listening to Him and ministering to Him in praise and worship.

"At this stage in my life, I am open and always listening to the Holy Spirit, wanting to respond in obedience to Him in whatever way He wants to move through me in prayer. It can happen at any place at any time, not just in my prayer closet.

"Fasting is about hearing the Lord more clearly and working hand in hand with Him at what He wants to accomplish. Fasting deals with oppression, the demonic or whatever else is intruding. God has a specific assignment during the fast. Through fasting, you're able to focus on that situation under His guidance."

Pearl experienced several breakthroughs as a result of fasting.

"Sometimes God will give me the names of people and impressions while I'm praying. This only comes through the discipline of reading the Bible, prayer and fasting.

"I did my first ten day water fast when I was in Bible school and quickly learned that fasting brings breakthroughs. At that time, my father was facing several serious and false accusations at work. They wanted to put him in prison. After ten days of fasting and prayer, his name was cleared.

"When I moved here, I had no one to help me get established. I started a twenty-one-day juice fast and sought the Lord's help and guidance. It wasn't long and I found a job.

"In July, I went on a twenty-five-day water fast. It really changed me, giving me a greater heart, hunger and love for God. I had been spiritually struggling and copying others instead of being with God. Fasting helped break the negative patterns and bring me to a new level in my relationship with Him. After fasting, the things I used to want, I didn't desire anymore. All the idols I had allowed to take hold in my life seemed to be removed.

> *Sometimes one word from God will change everything.*

"Fasting also keeps me sensitive to hearing God's voice. He speaks the clearest to me through the Bible, telling me the things I need to hear, not necessarily the things I want to hear."

Sharon said,

"I often read about past revivalists. The common element in their lives was prayer and fasting, even praying through the night. Sometimes there was only one or two of them praying together.

"I am in awe of what people sacrificed and the fruit which resulted. I want to see God raise that pioneering spirit up again. Those pioneers in the faith pressed into the Lord, seeking His face and hungering for Him. We don't see a lot of that anymore.

"One time, God called me to do an Esther Fast. The first day was the hardest, but the rest was a breeze. It was God initiated and I saw the fruit of it. Recently I was doing another three day fast. Our son was home working during the day with my husband. I knew he would be here for supper with us and wondered what I should do. God said, 'Eat supper with your son!' God is so practical.

"Looking back over the years, I firmly believe that fasting was part of God's protection over us and a major factor in dealing with the self issues we all face.

"When God was first getting me into fasting and prayer, I believed that we literally could live on the Word of God. Science tells us we can't. However, God knows what we need and when. Moses and Jesus were human beings and God supernaturally intervened for them during fasting.

"There will always be an attack from the enemy to keep us from prayer and especially from fasting. Jim Cymbala believes that if the apostles could see Christians now, they would shake their heads in disbelief.

"Several years ago, there was an important meeting regarding the school. Everyone knew it would be volatile. God put it on the heart of a group of us to fast breakfast on the day of the meeting. The meeting was peaceful, friendly, and in complete agreement, a visible result of fasting for only one meal."

Amanda ^{C.} shared,

"While I was still in high school, I was trying to learn more about spiritual growth and considered taking one day every week for fasting. My grandma had a book on fasting that I read and tried to abstain from food and water for an entire day. When I became more used to this, I considered taking one day every week for fasting, but I didn't keep going. I kept trying and will fast periodically without food for a full day.

"What I've found most beneficial is a media fast. After I spend a chunk of time away from social media, I obtain more spiritual clarity and focus and don't want to go back.

"Several years ago after finishing a social media fast, I felt like I should continue, but expand it to other areas. I started eliminating things like junk food and extra sugars from my diet. After that, I began a Daniel fast which lasted for several months. I would also take certain lunch hours to pray instead of eating. As I fasted for prayer and spiritual reasons, I became healthier physically. Over time my metabolism was corrected.

"After I was married, we were invited to foreign missions, but I wasn't hearing God in the same way then. After seeking God through fasting and prayer, I felt Him clearly say that He was inviting us to go, though we didn't have to. Through fasting and prayer, I have noticed being able to hear God more clearly and experienced increased intimacy with Him.

"I knew I wanted to be a part of the revival I felt God was bringing to that closed nation; preparing the way for revival through prayer was a God opportunity. We left everything behind and became full-time workers. Although we knew God was inviting us to go, several months later, we didn't hear Him tell us to stay. We returned to Canada after four months of ministering in the prayer room."

Jewell also combined fasting with prayer.

"I don't fast from food but have felt God lead me to fast from talking, where I stop speaking for a couple of days. It is very powerful. For some people, food may be an interruption, but for me, all the babbling and chatter is more of an interruption to my thoughts and prayers.

"I was seeking God for answers to a specific family situation. Not speaking to others allowed me to become intimate with God. God doesn't need our voice in communication.

"I cut off all outside distractions including music, television, or anything that had a vocal element. When you have four kids and a husband, silence isn't an option, so I had to go away from home for that kind of a fast."

Patrick says,

"My prayers include praying for God's purpose and calling on my life. My wife and I are pressing in for our purpose. I take advantage that I can choose to fast. God is drawing me to fast as I am pressing in for certain things at school, in my marriage and for ministry.

"There is usually a delayed breakthrough that results from fasting. Something changes. Yes, there is external fruit, but something changes internally as well. There are often changes I don't necessarily recognize. We had a prayer and fasting week at school, and we experienced noticeable changes. Yet those changes were hard to put your finger on and explain fully.

"I've heard and read testimonies of others fasting and experiencing more angelic type encounters. I've noticed that to be true for me as well."

Allison's perspective about fasting is important to consider as well.

"Fasting is a wonderful gift of God because it crushes any claim to power that we have apart from Him. All sense of authority we think we have in ourselves must humble itself before the authority of Christ. How do we humble ourselves? We fast. Unfortunately, fasting can in itself be turned into a means of pride.

"When we committed to an extended corporate fast at our church, I was all in. By day three, however, I was dizzy and passing out. The Lord said, 'You're done.'

"I argued with God, 'No, I'm not! What does that say about me and my spiritual state if I can't follow through with the fast?'

"It didn't take long though to submit to the Lord and start eating again. I felt guilty that everyone else was fasting but me. It taught me how the thing that was supposed to develop humility, actually became a source of pride at that moment.

"Recently, I applied for a university program, but the odds were definitely against me getting in. There was no natural way that I should obtain entrance into this university program. I had been reading in Daniel and felt the Lord invite me to a Daniel fast. After praying about it, I decided to fast similar to that of Daniel and his companions when they were preparing to come into the king's court. As I fasted, I continued to meditate on the Scriptures in Daniel. It was a powerful time for me to personally draw close to the Lord, leaning on Him and believing that what He did for Daniel He would do for me. I knew the favor of God that rested on Daniel was also resting on me.

"Even though I shortened the length of the fast because of my involvement in ministry trips, fasting helped me to lean into God through prayer. I was able to give back to the Lord any worry about unfulfilled desires about wanting to enter the program. The fact I was granted enrolment was an amazing miracle. It was a miracle not because of the fast, but because of God's faithfulness.

"There is a grace for fasting not based on our works so that none of us can boast. It's not based on *my* faith, but it's an obedience walk. The most important thing for me is to continually pray from a soft heart to discern what God is asking for each season I'm in."

Helen wanted to see a miracle; the miracle she received was unexpected.

"I couldn't fast intensively because of health issues. One time I fasted for three days because I was asking God for a miracle in my life. At the end of three days, my husband came to the Lord.

"I didn't know what I was asking when I prayed, 'All I want is for You to do a miracle in my life.'

"We were living in a house with one of those big television dishes in the back yard. All we could view on television were cartoons and a Gospel channel called *"Praise the Lord."* Every night, it seemed like my husband would be watching. I couldn't believe it! Then one night he prayed the sinner's prayer with R.W. Shambach.

"I questioned, 'Is this real, God?' It was real; God's hand was on both of our lives so clearly."

Unlocking the Legacy

Isaiah, perhaps more than any other prophet, succinctly articulated God's design and purpose for fasting, devoting an entire chapter to the subject. He reprimands those who thought that by denying themselves food they could convince God to do what they wanted, how they wanted.

I'm all too guilty of the same attitudes, unfortunately. I falsely think, "Since God hasn't answered prayer alone, I'll fast. That will persuade Him." Wrong motivation!

Fasting, like everything else in our spiritual lives, is based on intimacy—drawing close to God in love. Ultimately, intimacy aligns our hearts with God's heart, leading us to intercede as He desires. Out of this place of intimate communion with Him, we pray and move in agreement with His perfect will where answers are found.

> **"Is not this the kind of fasting I have chosen:**
> **to loose the chains of injustice and untie the cords**
> **of the yoke, to set the oppressed free and break**
> **every yoke? Is it not to share your food with the**
> **hungry and to provide the poor wanderer with shel-**
> **ter—when you see the naked, to clothe them,**
> **and not to turn away from your own flesh and**
> **blood?** *Then* **your light will break forth like the**
> **dawn, and your healing will quickly appear;**
> *then* **your righteousness will go before you, and the**
> **glory of the LORD will be your rear guard.** *Then*
> **you will call, and the LORD will answer; You will**
> **cry for help, and he will say, Here am I."**
> **Isaiah 58:6-9**
> **(Emphasis mine)**

Isaiah explains that fasting is a form of prayer which actively pursues resolution for the needs of others while breaking off oppressive yokes of bondage that deprive people of God's blessing and provision.

Fasting is meant to **"loose the chains...untie the cords... and set the oppressed free."**

Not only does fasting bring deliverance for those around us, but also personal change:

> our light shines brighter;
>> our healing appears;
>>> our righteousness precedes us;
>>>> and our prayers are answered.

> *"I believe that fasting as it relates to prayer is the spiritual atomic bomb that the Lord has given us to destroy the strongholds of evil and usher in a great revival and spiritual harvest around the world."* [1]

This atomic-like force released through prayer and fasting cannot be denied or disqualified scripturally or practically.

Jesus pointed His listeners back to the primary purpose of fasting, which is intimacy with God. Fasting has always been a recognized practice for those seeking more of God's presence. The Pharisees of Jesus' day fasted, as did the disciples of John the Baptist. They wondered why Jesus' followers did not.

> **"Jesus answered, 'How can the guests of the bridegroom mourn while he is with them? The time will come when the bridegroom will be taken from them; then they will fast."**
> **Matthew 9:15**

When Jesus spoke these words, He was
> tangibly present,
>> intimately involved,
>>> reachable and touchable,
>>>> seen, heard and known.

With intimacy as a daily reality, fasting was unnecessary. However, when He left this earth's domain and returned to Heaven, fasting became imperative to experience Jesus again as
> tangibly present,
>> intimately involved,
>>> reachable and touchable,

seen, heard and known to those who earnestly seek Him.

Jesus was led into the wilderness by the Holy Spirit into a forty-day fast before embarking on His ministry (Mt 4:1-2). Esther fasted as preparation to enter the king's presence on behalf of her people (Est 4:15-17). Moses fasted while receiving God's law (Ex 34:28). Daniel fasted for revelation (Dan 10:1-3).

When enemy forces pressed in, Jehoshaphat called a national fast and people **"came from every town"** to seek God and His help (2 Chr 20:3-4). Perhaps, this type of fast is most relatable for us. When we know that nobody but God can intervene, we lay aside even the most basic of needs to seek His face and direction. When we do, as with Jehoshaphat, we find Him present and powerful.

It's true, fasting subdues the desires of the flesh under the Holy Spirit's authority. No matter the proven health benefits to fasting, the goal for biblical fasting aims far beyond the physical realm.

Fasting prepares and equips us militarily for defeating the enemy while simultaneously connecting us to the Commander and Chief of Heaven's army in an intimate and personal way. Fasting creates dramatic change outwardly and inwardly.

It is here in the place of deep intimacy, God hands us the key to unlocking legacy. Without this key of fasting, we will miss the intentions of God's heart and lose the treasures revealed only through intimacy.

Sharon found God to be practical. Many people cannot fast from food for physical reasons, but we can all fast from something. As we seek God, He will show us what is robbing us of time and intimacy with Him. Perhaps it will be a silent fast, turning off every voice but God's. It might be a media fast, denying the influence of the world. My grand-daughter fasted for forty days from playing with her favorite toys.

The how of the fasting isn't as critical as the purpose. When we intend to seek God's face and His heart, He will show Himself clearly and powerfully to us.

Don't hesitate! The ability to break off bondages comes to those who pray and fast (Mk 9:29). Let's pick up the key marked *fasting* to unlock the legacy that has remained hidden and bound.

Taking Territory

"Father, whether You call us to fast one meal, one day, a week or longer may we respond with a willing and submissive heart. You know the areas in our lives that resist Your authority and bend too easily under the influence of others. God, direct us into biblical fasting so that we would see Your Kingdom come and Your will be done on Earth.

" **'As the deer pants for streams of water, so our soul pants for You . . . Our soul thirsts for (You), God, (our) living God . . . (may our) tears before You be (our) food day and night'** (Ps 42:1-3).

"We long for You with an unquenchable hunger and thirst. God, draw us into a time of fasting and prayer that will awaken our need for You only. We confess that we are too easily pacified by comfort and ease. Give us hearts willing to go without temporary things so You can be released to bring permanent transformational change.

"Lord, open our eyes to see the desperate needs of those still held captive in enemy territory. May we be sensitive to the cries of the needy and the oppressed. Forgive us for turning our backs for so long on the hurting and desperate.

"We confess that we want to experience the benefits of fasting without the pain of denying our flesh. Too often, we want Your light to shine brightly through us into our world without personal sacrifice.

"We long to see Your power released and Your Presence to be made known as demons flee, blinded eyes see, cancers eradicated and limbs restored, resources transferred into Your Kingdom purposes, and the bondages of addictions broken. Is our apathy toward fasting reflective of our impotence in prayer? If so, change us!

"When the disciples couldn't cast out a demon, Jesus said, **'This kind can come out only by prayer and fasting'** (Mk 9:29). We acknowledge that there is a legacy of freedom only available through the diligent pursuit of You through prayer and fasting. May we not settle for a little when there is so much more accessible through the key of fasting.

"Here we are Lord, use us as You desire. May we be drawn into seasons of fasting not out of our own initiative, but led by Holy Spirit. Prepare us through fasting

for new ministry opportunities,

to receive divine revelation and understanding,

to stand in the gap for our nation and people,

to discern how and when to speak,

to yield ourselves entirely for Your purposes,

standing against injustice and discrimination,

generously meeting the practical needs of others.

"May our ears become sensitive to Your voice of instruction as we submit ourselves to fasting. Thank You, Lord, for freely giving us every key we need to unlock our legacy. May we have an urgency and desire for breakthrough great enough to pursue it. Fasting and humility are teammates, comrades in battle, partners in exploits. Use fasting to bring every aspect of our lives into full surrender to Your will.

"Forgive us for postponing fasting for desperate seasons, or relegating it to a radical few. We come today seeking Your face and a deeper intimacy attainable only through fasting. Reveal Your purpose and establish Your plan for denying our flesh and feeding our spirit.

"We long for You to be clearly seen and known. May Your Name be honored and lifted high. Whatever it takes, may we cooperate with Holy Spirit to bring You glory and praise.

" 'We return to (You) with all (our) hearts, with fasting, weeping and mourning,' drawing close to You, Lord (Jl 2:12). As we do, the church will be clothed in Your glory and majesty, rising in strength, dignity and power, presenting herself to You 'without stain or wrinkle or any other blemish, but holy and blameless' (Eph 5:27).

"Thank You! We lay hold of the legacy You have waiting for us.

Amen."

> *"God's accounting is not day to day or month to month; it might be decade to decade. Perseverance goes with fasting as we press in." — Clay*

***

> "*Until the church decides they are going to fast and pray, nothing will change. The price for success is paid in prayer and fasting.*" – *Caleb*

***

> "*Fasting allows me to be more in tune with God. It opens my spirit to know what God is wanting for today.*" – *Mark*

***

Notes

1. Bill Bright, 7 Basic Steps to Successful Fasting and Prayer, cru.org, https://www.cru.org/us/en/train-and-grow/spiritual-growth/fasting/7-steps-to-fasting.html.

CHAPTER 9

Operating in Authority
– Equipped for Battle

> *"Instead of worrying about the smoke coming out of the enemy's camp, pray for Kingdom perspective and with Kingdom authority."*
> — Heather

The dreaded day had arrived. Earth and sky converged together as clouds pressed so low one felt they could be touched. Even the sun refused to show its face.

Hope seemed to vanish as swift as the rain rushing, swirling and disappearing down the gutters to unseen places, never to return. I trudged up the outer steps and passed security, before following the polished floors of the spacious hallway leading toward two massive oak doors. Entering quietly, I found an inconspicuous seat near the back of the large, hollow room.

A muffled cough only slightly creased the weighty silence hanging over the witnesses. Dread and despondency drooped low within the chamber, mimicking the slouching clouds in the streets outside. Blank stares marked the somber faces of the many huddled here.

"What are their stories? Who are they?" Quickly I swept my questions aside, trying not to think, not to wonder, not to care. Today, the cost of compassion for total strangers held a price far surpassing what I could pay.

"All rise," a voice demanded. "The court is now in session. Honorable Judge Jacobs presiding."

This wasn't the first time I stood in a court of law. I understood clearly that the judge represented ultimate authority here in the court-room and expanded to the law itself. Waiting for the judge to take his position, everyone stood respectfully before settling back into their places. The almost theatrical formalities of the courtroom seemed to amplify the sense of powerlessness I felt in this unfamiliar domain.

After listening to a series of other trials, my young defendant was called. "Please state your name."

"C___ B___ V___," she stated.

"Do you swear that the testimony you are about to give is the truth, the whole truth, and nothing but the truth?"

"Yes, your Honor," she responded. Her voice attempted to portray confidence she lacked, a surety she wished she possessed.

The list of charges read against her was longer than I had hoped, more serious than I previously thought. I fought back the tears of shared sorrow as she confessed, "Guilty on all accounts, your Honor." The truth of the charges eviscerated excuse, decimated denial and annihilated all claim to innocence.

My mind had difficulty focusing on the judge as he emphasized the seriousness of the charges filed against her. With all the authority vested in him, he declared to her and the entire courtroom, "I hereby sentence you to three years in prison beginning immediately." With one stroke of the gavel, the verdict had been given. Justice had been served. Or had it?

Fighting back tears, I watched as guards methodically escorted her from the courtroom.

Suddenly, it was as if I was transported to another court yet to be. This time, it was me, thrust cuffed and shackled, on my knees before the Judge of all ages. The long, almost endless, list of charges I had committed was shown on a massive high-definition screen for all to see. Solemnly, I listened. Remorse gripped me denying me voice.

Sitting upon His throne surrounded by blazing light and fire, He asked, "How do you plead?"

With head bowed, afraid to gaze in the direction of perfect Holiness, I waited in stunned silence; the accuracy of each charge was blindingly obvious. Plead? How could one possibly plead?

Confidently, the Son entered, boldly striding toward the throne and the One sitting on it. Jesus Christ, my Advocate, stood strong and resolute before the Judge. He didn't come empty-handed but brought with Him His own shed blood. "Not guilty, Your Honor. This one is mine. She has been bought at the highest price. I declare her not guilty!"

A dark, shadowy figure, defiant and scowling, leaped to his feet seething, "What! How? Repeatedly, she has defiled herself—blatantly betraying You." He stumbled over his words, emphasizing and slurring them as he glared in disdain at no one and yet everyone all at the same time. "Look at her, covered in shame and shrouded in lies. She neither looks, sounds nor acts like You. How can she possibly be yours?"

"Silence!" the Judge roared. At the sound of His thunderous voice, the accuser slithered away, unapologetically.

The charges were true, the evidence real. The accuser was accurate on every violation of the law. How greatly I had failed to obey and follow the One who had redeemed me. Yet here My Savior stood between me, a wretched sinner, and Holy God, interceding on my behalf. He turned and moved deliberately toward me. While draping my shoulders with pure white linen, He spoke again loud enough for everyone to hear. "She is mine—righteous, innocent and blameless. Not guilty, Your Honor." Taking my hand in His, He brought me face to face before the throne of the perfect and Righteous Judge.

The sound of the gavel casting another verdict and ending another preceding jolted me back to the present. The courtroom, both now and then, is a perfect representation of power and authority. Psalms 89:14 echoed in the chambers of my heart as I rose quietly to leave, **"Righteousness and justice are the foundation of your throne; love and faithfulness go before you."**

Through the years there would be many other court cases to attend, but this one would forever change my perspective of God's authority to bring judgment based on the law and our authority as His children walking, living and praying in the light of everything Jesus Christ has done.

151

Many times since that day, I have stood with authority against the accuser while positioned on my knees in prayer. Jesus Christ, as my Advocate and Intercessor, covers me in righteousness to come before His Father and mine. Confidently I approach; boldly I seek. This is the place of mercy and grace.

Personal Perspectives

Dawn is a true warrior in prayer.

"When I get to the point of no distractions and am absolutely being truthful about whatever is on my heart, that to me is praying in the Spirit. I know that I am speaking to Him and have made it to the throne room. I know He hears me. I don't pray or speak in tongues.

"Recently, I've known I was doing battle in prayer. We left a short-term mission position; I felt unsettled and lacked peace. I was upset feeling like we had lost favor with all our leadership.

"I felt God tell me to turn off the television and deal with my feelings. I knew I had been striving for approval. God was working it out of me. I battled through in prayer, sitting and weeping before the Lord, asking Him the hard questions as to why the acceptance of others mattered so much to me.

> *If this was the enemy, I didn't want to play his game.*

"It was hurting me to the point that I never wanted to go back to church again. I didn't know how to get through. God showed me that ultimately, in both instances, I was fighting the same thing.

"Numbers 10 reminded me that when we take territory that

the enemy has encroached on, we are to blow the trumpet. I didn't link everything together until the next morning in prayer. In the short term mission. I had taken the territory called 'obedience' from the enemy. Now, he was trying to push me back and say, 'No! This is not your land.'

"God reminded me that I *was* His obedient child. He showed me how striving for approval falls away when I have His favor. We have to get our eyes off each other and unto Jesus. God has individual and corporate work for each of us to do.

"I don't know what I'm doing when I am battling like that. I just know that I am doing something beyond me in God's authority."

Betty has had more than one tangle with the enemy.

"When our granddaughter was three days old, they found a tumor on her back. My father had died that same day. I was furious and yelling at the devil. I walked into the kitchen shouting, 'We know the end. Why don't you stop? God already told me this cancer will be for His glory.'

"The devil was getting mad too. Suddenly, I was airborne until I hit the cupboard several feet away. I landed on my butt laughing and thinking, 'Okay God, how am I going to get up.' I've had knee surgery so getting up from the floor is a problem.

"God said, 'Just roll yourself over to the entrance and use the railing.' Then He gave me a word,

> *When the devil whispers that the storm is too big for you, you whisper, 'I am a woman of faith and a child of God. I am the storm.'*

"When the devil knows that you know who you are, he's scared! He can't hurt you unless you allow it. It was a big revelation for me. That's the third time the devil has sent me airborne and I've never been hurt.

"When God speaks and you know it is God, you don't have to wonder why something is taking a long time. Either you or the other person may be holding things up. God's timing is different from ours."

Keegan is also familiar with warfare.

"I have seen many miracles, all confirmed by doctors, right here in Canada: legs grow out, people in wheelchairs stand up, headaches and minor ailments healed. My friends have seen gold dust, smelled fresh, cooling oceanic breezes and other signs of God moving. At times, I've recognized the fragrance of the Lord too.

"I've been aware of demonic presences and have known it wasn't coming from the people around me. Even though my home was a safe place, as a child I had dreams of and an awareness of demonic presences in my room. I have prayed to see the more positive, but I think because I have a warrior spirit, I see demonic activity and oppression.

"Now as an adult, I understand my authority in Christ. Through really positive prophetic "dreams" when I am fully awake, God shows me the enemy's strategy and how to take His authority to help me overcome.

> *We have authority, but it doesn't come from ourselves or our desires.*

"The enemy usually tips his hand too much, yet it's subtle enough. He pushes us too hard into a corner, getting himself into trouble.

"In warfare, I often pace and speak in tongues. God shows me what needs to be done, often giving me a voice of command. Typically, I'm shy and fearful, not just to speak in public but generally. But when I started connecting with God and using my voice in warfare, I could sense the changes happening in me and around me. Whether I speak it out in prayer, give a shout of praise, sing, proclaim the words to a song, or wait quietly, I can always feel a spiritual shift.

"We have authority in Jesus' name. When we speak God's truth, we bind the enemy; the devil can't do anything against it. It is important to be tuned in with God, knowing what is needed at any moment.

"God will give us the wisdom to know what to do with a stronghold. We have to wait for God's direction to be sure He's calling us to take action, never confronting something that isn't ours to confront."

Emily knows her authority in prayer and spiritual warfare.

"I am reading through Joshua and learning about taking territory. We each have a territory God has given us: family, people He calls us to speak to, or whatever. God reveals things I don't necessarily want to see about the enemy, but it's all about taking territory.

> *Warfare is part of being a believer and tongues is the language of Heaven that the enemy doesn't understand.*

"God called Joshua to circumcise the people. Their obedience represented a circumcision of their hearts and removal of the reproach of Egypt, their enemy (Jo 5). Then He said, 'Fight!'

"God gave specific revelations for each battle. Joshua had to train up an army obedient to the Lord. Warfare is always a good thing when God is leading, but I am learning to wait on Him before I fight.

"Before it happened, God showed me that a friend of mine would become pregnant but would lose the baby without someone interceding. He led me by dreams, during the nine months she was pregnant, waking me up in the night and showing me how to intercede for her and the baby. I can't say that I always had confidence, but I spent those nine months warring in prayer for the baby's life.

"God has given me the gift of discernment, showing me the plans of the enemy even among those closest to me and revealing through dreams the bondages they are facing. I pray, trusting that God is working in their lives. I'm not the one working in their hearts; He is. I'm seeing a lot of fruit from what God is doing through warring intercession.

"Moses sent twelve spies into the promised land. Ten were doubters, but Joshua and Caleb had a different mindset. They were filled with faith and confidence that God would help them. **'We should go up and take possession of the land, for we can certainly do it,'** they said (Nm 13:30).

"At times, like the ten doubters, the first thing out of our mouths isn't positive. Don't be okay with it, but don't be hard on yourself either. It's a reality. We need to have high expectations while giving ourselves grace. In the hard times in prayer, we need to have the mind of Christ.

"Sometimes we have to keep praying for things, while at other times we pray once and know the answer is coming. We need to discern when it's time to fight and when to leave it with God, trusting Him.

"For me, warfare is often worshiping while playing the piano. Nehemiah told the people that the **'joy of the Lord is . . . strength'** (Neh 8:10). Where do we get strength from? Loving God. Where did it all start for us? Loving Him. Even during our battles, we need to come back to the place of relationship and loving Him."

(Note: The Hebrew word for strength is a military term *mā'ôg* meaning "God as a fortress...a shelter or strength...one's defense...stronghold or refuge."[1])

Heather discovered that her position of authority can also be the place of rest.

"I was praying against depression that always strikes at Christmas time. 'If the enemy can come in with depression, how much more can Your Spirit of light. Send Your angels of joy, Lord.'

"The next morning, I woke up with crushing suppression and crippling depression. I tried everything to overcome. By two o'clock in the afternoon, I crumbled. 'I just need You to come, Papa.' His presence instantly became so heavy.

"I felt Him say, 'Let's have a Daddy-daughter date.'

"I saw the image of junk food, so I went to the store to buy some. After eating it all, I immediately became extremely tired. 'I'm sorry Daddy for being such a terrible date.'

"Then I heard, 'There is no loving parent who doesn't like his child sitting on his lap.'

"I fell asleep on His lap. I was worshiping in that half-in-half-out kind of sleep, 'He causes me to triumph over my enemy . . .'

"I heard the Father's audible voice speaking His promises over my life. Whenever I woke up, He was still declaring, like He was reading a list, speaking His promises over me. I would fall back to sleep, then the song would come again and then His voice. This continued throughout the hour or two nap. God fought the battle for me while I slept.

"All my fighting and warring in prayer had done nothing. He desires to fight the battles for us. There is no demonic oppression He can't defeat.

We are not on the losing team!

"When nothing seems to be working, just do what He says. He prepares a banquet table for us in front of our enemies (Ps 23:5). I had a nap and He cleaned it up for me. God is so faithful. No word of God comes without the power to perform it (Lk 1:37). The words He speaks are rhema; they are words from Heaven that He will perform.

"The night before, I was praying by habit rather than listening to a rhema word. My warfare sounded like the mind of God. Instead of focusing on the enemy, God caused me to focus on something better, His presence."

Clay shared some insights he has learned about prayer.

"Prayer is a ministry of compassion. Even though some of our stories are horrendous, God has grace for our lives and stories. The enemy is alive and well. We are called to pray for individuals, communities, cities, districts and nations.

"Some of the prayer lessons I have learned have been quite unusual. Once, I was at a conference held in a beautiful area on the west coast, right on a mountain in an ocean inlet. We had one afternoon off and a local pastor asked if I would like to tour the area.

"He wanted to teach me how to pray for a community, so the first place he took me was to the cemetery. He went tombstone by tombstone, looking for historical facts and spiritual information or lack of it. Who was who? Whose tombstone was the largest?

"I have used that insight repeatedly when I go into a smaller community. If time permits, I will ask to be taken to the cemetery so I can prayer-walk there.

"In one local town, the old part of the cemetery had no mention of God on any tombstone—none, zero, zilch! The theme of the engravings said, 'I pulled myself up by the bootstraps. I did it my way.' There wasn't a single Christian saying. The original heritage held a godless, pioneer-cowboy kind of spirit. In the newer areas of the cemetery, Christian input was evident.

"I visited a graveyard at the other end of our nation. Again there was no mention of God anywhere. Interestingly, this community was the summer vacation spot for a notorious biker gang. While churches continuously struggled there, it consistently drew those from the dark side of life.

"I have learned to pray with discernment in three ways:

1. Keep your eyes open to know what is going on around you.
2. Know the Word of God to know what is right and wrong spiritually.
3. Recognize what God is currently imprinting on your mind.

"While listening and observing those kinds of things, I was invited to assist another small church. We went through the cemetery praying before the conference. One name on a tombstone seemed to pop out at me. It marked the death of a baby only one day old. I thought, 'That would have been so sad.' That's all I picked up as we prayed.

"That morning at the church, we talked about painful memories. No one shared anything; it was quiet. I sensed pride was a stronghold. God brought the image of that little grave-stone back to my mind. There was someone in the church with the same name, so I said, 'That must have been painful back in the 1930s when that happened.'

"An older lady put up her hand. 'I lost my baby during the depression when things were tough. We buried the baby, but I had to keep working in the field. She started weeping. That broke the dam; everyone shared painful memories.

> *Warfare prayer is about being observant, knowing what is going on around us, and seeking God's directive.*

"Years ago, we did spiritual mapping in our city. There was a grove of trees in an area that had been used for Wicca cere-monies. We prayed for God to redeem the land. Twenty years later, the trees were torn down and it has become productive and useful. God's accounting may take time, but He comes through.

"Wicca people also sacrificed animals and stuff on the door-steps of a church in our community. The secretary, who was spiritually sensitive and concerned, asked us to come and pray. The pastor, however, wanted nothing to do with it and immediately fired her. As we prayed, we zeroed in on some history, discovering that there was an abandoned farm-house close by also used for these ceremonies. We prayed through the situation and the church didn't have any more problems with sacrifices.

"That occurred about twenty-five years ago. Recently, the city donated the farmland and a Christian owned company has built an elementary school on the property.

"One of my favorite Bible stories is of the centurion who came to Jesus. Jesus said, 'I will come and help your son.' The centurion, who understood authority, replied, 'Don't bother coming, just say the word.' Jesus commended him, **'No greater faith have I found in all of Israel'** (Lk 7:10).

"The connection between faith and authority is the key to warfare prayer. When we have permission to go and pray, it's our ground, our land, and our facility. We can clean house! If we don't have permission, we can only pray *for* them. Authority is key.

"Many people are seeking the power of God. God has already given us power and authority, but if we are outside our level of authority, we waste our prayers. We never fully know what God will use in our prayers and lives. We just pray with faith, authority and power."

> *In terms of having power and authority, confession and a willing heart are key.*

Charlene shared,

"About nine years ago, I felt the Lord say that He had given us a place of authority over our community. Even though we had already been here for several years, there was a specific time when we gained authority. I don't know what we did or what shifted and changed. I felt I had to speak that out loud as a declaration, so I did.

"Five more years passed before a significant aspect of moving in authority came into fruition. There was a situation with the government of our community. People were asking us to pray for the hospitals, schools, teachers, and police. I know a lot of teaching tells us we have authority in those areas and we should pray that way, but we never stepped into it.

"All of a sudden, our community was dealing with a situation that we felt it didn't have to be dealing with. Everybody knew what was going on. We also knew that God loved our community—these were people He created. We knew we had the authority to pray.

> *We always pray from a God of mercy, that He would show His love, and they would come to Christ.*

"We listened to the Spirit's direction. We prayed that everyone would repent and turn to the Lord but asked God to remove those who wouldn't repent.

"In a short time, God turned everything around."

Unlocking the Legacy

Don't be deceived! A battle is raging! We aren't ignorant of the enemies' schemes, plans and devices (2 Cor 2:11).

**"For our struggle is not against flesh and blood,
but against the rulers, against the authorities,
against the powers of this dark world and against
the spiritual forces of evil in the Heavenly realms."
Ephesians 6:12**

There is no reason to fear or become discouraged in battle. The war has already been won. Jesus Christ has crushed the head of satan at the cross. As we walk in our God-given authority we follow behind Him, sweeping the remains out of the way.

After Jesus was baptized, He was led by the Holy Spirit into the wilderness. Only then could and would His ministry begin.

> *"One Jesus walked into the wilderness, but another*
> *Jesus came out of the wilderness with a different mantle,*
> *a different authority, a different way of speaking. He*
> *had such power and authority that a whole geographical*
> *area began to talk about Him."* [2]

Throughout His earthly ministry, Jesus functioned within the fullness of the authority God had given Him. Just before He ascended into Heaven, He said,

> **"*All authority* in Heaven and on earth has been**
> **given to me. Therefore go and make disciples of all**
> **nations, baptizing them in the name of the Father**
> **and of the Son and of the Holy Spirit, and teaching**
> **them to obey everything I have commanded you.**
> **And surely I am with you always, to the**
> **very end of the age."**
> **Matthew 28:18-20**
> **(Emphasis mine)**

Luke writes,

> **"But** *you will receive power* **when the**
> **Holy Spirit comes on you; and you will be**
> **my witnesses in Jerusalem, and in all Judea and**
> **Samaria, and to the ends of the earth."**
> **Acts 1:8**
> **(Emphasis mine)**

These instructions were an extension of what Jesus' followers had experienced previously. Jesus gave His disciples both **"power and authority to drive out all demons and to cure diseases, and he sent them out to proclaim the kingdom of God and to heal the sick"** (Lk 9:1-2). Power, or *dunamis*, speaks of the miraculous power of signs and wonders.[3] However, authority, or *exousia*, refers to permission, right or liberty. *Exousia* denies the presence of any hindrance and may be used either of the capability or the right to do a certain thing. It is a combination of right and might.[4]

Since the fall of mankind, satan operates as a rebel holder of authority. Through the cross and resurrection he still has power, but Jesus Christ has stripped him of all the authority he once held. Jesus now possesses supreme power and complete authority. What is more astounding is that as co-heirs with Christ, He has granted us the right and the might to operate in His power and authority—not independent of Him, but rather cooperating with Him to do His will on earth.

Power is the ability to rule; authority is the right to rule. God has raised us and seated us with Him in the place of authority in the Heavenly realm (Eph 2:6). That is where we already are positioned. In prayer and intercession, we recognize our rightful position in Christ. We come boldly before "**God's throne of grace with confidence, so that we may receive mercy and find grace to help us in our time of need**" (Heb 4:16).

Perhaps no other key to unlocking legacy is as potently strategic as knowing the authority we have in Jesus Christ before God's throne. Every praying believer must understand the authority they possess in Christ and the power they obtain from submitting to Him.

When the people of Israel were hemmed in with the Red Sea in front and the Egyptian army pressing in from behind, at God's command Moses stood in the Lord's authority. "**Raise your staff and stretch out your hand over the sea to divide the water so that the Israelites can go through the sea on dry ground**" (Ex 14:17). Moses' staff was a symbol of divine authority as he positioned himself to intercede.

Jehoshaphat called a national fast to seek God's help when a military coalition advanced against them. He assigned singers to go ahead of the army. "**You will not have to fight this battle. Take up your positions; stand firm and see the deliverance the LORD will give you . . . go out to face them . . . and the LORD will be with you**" (2 Chr 20:17). As worshipers of the Most High God, they knew the authority they possessed. Earthly weapons were unnecessary. Their voices of praise threw the enemy into chaos.

An angel spoke to Zechariah in a vision, " . . . '**Not by might nor by power, but by my Spirit,' says the LORD Almighty (Zec 4:6).' **" Solid words of truth then and now!

Our battle against the adversary isn't a power struggle. If it was, we would lose. Remember, he still holds power. We, however, have both power and authority in the courts of Heaven. Jehoshaphat knew the battle against the enemy wasn't about power, but rather authority. **"Our eyes are on you,"** he said to the Lord (2 Chr 20:12).

When we are willing to assume our position, raising our voices in prayer, we too will see God

    make a way where there is no way,

        throw confusion into the enemy camp,

            acquit the innocent and charge the guilty,

  bring justice and righteousness to our cause,

        heal the sick, raise the dead and cast out demons,

           effectively declare the Gospel to all nations.

In prayer, our eyes are on God and Him alone. We look to our Advocate, Jesus Christ, and come boldly before the throne of grace, finding grace to help us in our time of need (Heb 4:16).

"Intercessory prayer requires identification with the one who is interceded for, agony to feel the burden, and authority in Christ." [5]

On our knees, we stand. On our faces, we take up our positions.

"And [I pray] that the eyes of your heart [the very center and core of your being] may be enlightened [flooded with light by the Holy Spirit], so that you will know and cherish the hope [the divine guarantee, the confident expectation] to which He has called you, the riches of His glorious inheritance in the saints (God's people), and [so that you will begin to know] what the immeasurable and unlimited and surpassing greatness of His [active spiritual] power is in us who believe. These are in accordance with the working of His mighty strength."
Ephesians 1:18-19 AMP

We have been given power and authority—an invincible combination—to unlock godly legacy and secure our inheritance.

Taking Territory

"Lord Jesus, You did not come to abolish the law but to fulfill every requirement of it (Mt 5:17). As Great High Priest, You understand our weakness and have made a way for us to come before God's throne (Heb 4:14-16). We come boldly in prayer appealing to our Father for grace, mercy and help. We ask for ourselves and others.

"Lord, we do not come demanding anything of You. Rather, we come in humility, by Your grace and Your grace alone—not on our own merits but based on what You have done on the cross.

"You are our Advocate before the Father, declaring us as Your own and righteous in Your sight (1 Jn 2:1-2). I thank You that now You are making intercession on our behalf (Heb 7:25). **'Even now my witness is in Heaven; my advocate is on high. My intercessor is my friend as my eyes pour out tears to God; on behalf of a man he pleads with God as one pleads for a friend'** (Jb 16:19-21). We are Your children, heirs and co-heirs, seated with You in Heavenly places (Rom 8:17, Eph 2:6).

"Thank You for giving us both the power and authority to extend Your Kingdom here on Earth. We are neither fragile nor weak. **'For though we live in the world, we do not wage war as the world does. The weapons we fight with are not the weapons of the world. On the contrary, they have divine power to demolish strongholds. We demolish arguments and every pretension that sets itself up against the knowledge of God, and we take captive every thought to make it obedient to Christ'** (2 Cor 10:3-5). We come into agreement with what You have declared about us and for us.

"On our knees in prayer, we stand. On our faces in intercession, we take up our positions. Prostrate we bow. O God, we confess, **'we do not know what to do, but our eyes are on you'** (2 Chr 20:12).

"We will not be distracted by the subtle insinuations or raging outbursts of the accuser. We humble ourselves under Your mighty hand, staying alert and sober-minded, resisting the devil and all his cohorts

(1 Pt 5:6-9).

"Your **'divine power has given us everything we need for a god- ly life through our knowledge of him who called us by his own glory and goodness. Through these (You) have given us (Your) very great and precious promises . . .'** (2 Pt 1:3-4).

"We lack nothing! Everything we need, You have given to us. We will not boast in the exploits of battle but in the Name of the Lord. You have written our names in Heaven and on the very palms of your hands (Lk 10:20, Is 49:16).

"We take the keys of power and authority unlocking the legacy before us. Apart from You, we can do nothing (Jn 15:5); with You, all things are possible (Mt 19:26). In the Name of the Lord Jesus Christ, we legitimately take hold of the keys of authority. We set our faces like flint to do Your will.

"In Your Name, we cast out demons, cure diseases, and pro- claim the Kingdom of God to all nations (Lk 9:1-2). In prayer, we run with the swift and fight with the strong. Our **'help comes from the Lord, the Maker of Heaven and earth'** (Ps 121:2).

"Our legacy is waiting to be unlocked. The courts have ruled in our favor. The enemy has been disarmed and stripped of all authority. We follow our Victor, Jesus Christ, picking up the spoils of battle He has already won.

"Thank You, Jesus. We love You, Lord.

Amen."

> *"My husband walks in authority and knows his position of authority. He prays and POOF!"*
> *– Charlene*

***

> *"I was shocked to realize the majority of Christians are not necessarily praying Christians.*
> *Prayer was what God put on me and was doing in me, giving me a warrior spirit."*
> *— Sharon*

***

> *"God askes me to partner with Him.*
> *We have authority with the Father in sonship."*
> *— Emmanuel*

***

Notes

1. Warren Baker, D.R.E and Eugene Carpenter, Ph.D., ed., *Complete Word Study Dictionary: Old Testament: For a Deeper Understanding of The Word* (Chattanooga, AMG Publishers, 2003), 639.
2. Rachel Hickson, *Little Keys Open Big Doors: Secrets to Experiencing Breakthrough in Every Area of Life* (Grand Rapids, Chosen Books, 2007), 211.
3. Spiros Zodhiates Th.D., ed., *The Complete Word Study Dictionary: New Testament: For a Deeper Understanding of the Word*, rev. ed., (Chattanooga, AMG International Inc., 1993), 485.
4. Zodhiates, *The Complete Word Study Dictionary: New Testament*, 607.
5. Frank Damazio, *From Barrenness to Fruitfulness: Restoration for the Heart and Soul of Leaders*, (Ventura, Regal Books, 1998), 87.

CHAPTER 10

Two or Three are Gathered – Praying Together

> *"When a group of believers is in agreement, in unity with like mind and one accord before the Lord, that is huge. God will command a blessing."*
> *– Kate*

As a member of the team committed to garrison ourselves around this little life in prayer, we were thrust into action with the succinct message.

"Heading to the hospital now. Baby being induced."

Complications developed during the pregnancy and in wisdom the mother enlisted prayer recruits early, giving updated progress reports regularly. She sensed the unction to build a multifaceted prayer force of thirty plus intercessors during the pregnancy.

When the message arrived that morning, fasting was added to prayer until the delivery was complete. There were times of great peace in prayer, declaring God's sovereignty over the situation. Wisdom was needed by the physicians. In prayer, only gentle loving hands were invited to assist this little family.

The first day didn't go as planned. The mother was in extreme pain and made very little progress. The communication flowed infrequently between praying intercessors and the family. Words of encouragement, specific insights sensed through the Spirit, as well as progress reports were sporadically conveyed.

Hours past slowly—one day and night, then another day and another night ended without progress.

A brief text put us on high alert, "Emergency c section."

As I prayed, I saw the intercessors from Heaven's perspective as a circle of fully armed soldiers creating an impermeable barrier, encircling both mother and baby with protection. Some were bright and clearly visible; others appeared as faint shadows. I realized the more distinct warriors were those who were actively praying at that moment. The faint ones were resting, preparing to move forward at their prescribed time.

Then I saw a very large angel gently brush the mother's forehead with the tip of his powerful wing. Slowly and lovingly, He calmed and strengthened her as she laid before him in the delivery room.

In another area, several smaller angels hovered around something in the center of them. They rapidly moved in and out of position with authority and concentrated effort. The angels in this tiny circle moved with quick precision.

"Baby arrived. Keep praying."

The next day, more details came about the seriousness surrounding the delivery and the reasons for the urgency of the cesarean birth. The woman's mother was allowed into the birthing room for a few moments and was told, "Brush her forehead. That seems to comfort her."

Later, I also discovered that several skilled medical staff had worked on the baby resuscitating her lifeless body.

Astonished, I came to a realization that through intercessory prayer, Heaven and Earth were united in a single cohesive movement over mother and baby. What I saw angels do in the spirit realm, individuals were doing in the natural. As earth cooperated with Heaven, miracles happened that day.

Though there were many concerns over the next few days, this beautiful baby responded to life. She is now a busy little toddler with no complications or after-effects from an extended time without oxygen. There is wisdom in her eyes and brightness to her smile.

Later I wondered, "What would have happened if this young mother didn't include a prayer team in the birthing process? What if the intercessors would all have backed away after the first hour or day of prayer?"

There were numerable times when a member of the medical team, "just happened" to notice something, "just felt like" something else should be done. I am convinced that each decision was by Heaven's design. As people circled in the battle formation of prayer, shields were raised and swords were drawn. What easily looked like a tragedy in the making turned into a miracle of praise.

> *"Sometimes God answers in ways that appear so choreographed; it seems pre-choreographed. I think, 'Would this have happened even if I didn't pray?' In a sense, the answer was ready and waiting. Wow!"* — Christie

Personal Perspectives

During our interview, Allison shared,

"From the time I came into a personal relationship with the Lord, corporate prayer has been important. At a Tuesday evening intercessory prayer group, we studied prophetic prayer teachings by Dutch Sheets and others. The Wednesday morning prayer meeting was consistently attended by the same four or five people. Those meetings were the most powerful encounters with God I've ever had.

"I learned how to support others who were leading in prayer as we sought God together in the Spirit. We pressed into God's presence, wanting more of Him. We also developed trust in each other and faith in Holy Spirit speaking to us corporately. It was in that context I experienced many dimensions of prayer including travail and prophetic acts.

"No one said, 'I'm going to teach you how to pray.' People were committed to prayer and it was open for anybody to come and participate. As a new Christian, I was hungry to know God and enact my faith. I learned that corporate prayer was a part of what it meant to be a believer and assumed that's what all Christians did.

"A few years ago, I developed a relationship with a couple outside my denomination. They were dear people, fully devoted to the Lord, living out the Word and passionate about Jesus. This wife and I started meeting once a week for prayer. We would get together, read a psalm and start praying through it. It was rooted in Scripture and different than any type of prayer I was used to. Whatever Holy Spirit brought to our minds we prayed. It was such a precious, rich time in prayer—a sweet experience in the presence of the Lord. We would intercede for family members, a nation or however the Lord led.

> *Some kind of weekly corporate worship and prayer is essential for my spiritual health.*

"I need to make an effort personally to seek God through the Word, prayer, intercession, and worship, but also to engage in corporate prayer. Throughout my prayer seasons, these ways of seeking God have been my necessary benchmarks. No matter what season I am in, each one is important. Even if it is only for fifteen minutes daily by talking to the Lord and listening to Him, prayer needs to be part of my life."

Kate shares some of her experiences in corporate prayer.

"I felt drawn to seek out others who had the same prayer interests as I did. Praying out loud in a group was not comfortable initially. We would enjoy fellowship together as we prayed and worshiped the Lord. We prayed, cooperating and yielding to the Holy Spirit as a group. It was exciting.

"When God is in charge and we are all in like mind and Spirit, in one accord before Him, it is powerful. God commands His blessing when we seek Him with such unity."

Kristina discovered that corporate prayer has no boundaries.

"I enjoy praying in tongues. There's a cool story that happened about six years ago that kind of blew my mind.

"A friend of ours from church was pregnant. My husband, I, and our two children were on a holiday at the Mall of America at Minneapolis. Our friend's husband texted us, 'She's gone into labor, please pray.'

"I don't know if the kids were in strollers, but Michael and I walked around inside the corridors of the mall, quietly praying in tongues for this friend who was in active labor. The baby was born and all was well.

"Later, when we were back home, she told me that when she was in labor, she could hear my voice praying in tongues. She could hear me! We were out of the country and she could hear me praying in tongues.

"That blew my mind in terms of what happens when we pray in tongues."

355

Charlene talked about the process of creating a culture of prayer.

"I had been involved in many prayer groups, but when we moved, we were planted into a very different prayer culture. I thought I needed to transition everything into the new group from the culture I had come from. Yet, the Holy Spirit was moving us into something else. I've learned massive amounts while training up others who don't have any misconceptions about prayer.

"You don't walk away from praying the Word of God and listening for prophetic answers through prayer. You don't walk away from praying in the Spirit, as it becomes tongues and interpretation. You don't leave travail either.

"We had brand new believers and we had to teach them how to pray, starting with our hearts. If our hearts aren't right, we don't have the boldness to pray or the ability to hear well. We learned as a group to listen to Holy Spirit and pray as He directed. We felt that we should always start with worship and realized if we did nothing else but worship, we had prayed.

"That's hard because we live in a culture which asks, 'What did you accomplish?'

" 'We worshipped!'

"I told the group that it was going to be an eight-week course because I didn't think they could commit to anything longer. It ended up being twelve weeks long. Everyone we mentored is still part of our Tuesday prayer.

"I had to learn authority.
I had to learn the Word.
I had to learn travail.
I had to learn how to hear prophetically.

Then I had to learn to put it all together and let God govern our prayer meetings.

"It isn't that we all think the same way, but we all operate under the same principles of listening to what the Holy Spirit is saying: 'When do You want us to pray about this? How do You want us to pray about that? Is there anything we are supposed to do here?'

"It's not that we don't want to pray for Aunt Julie's toe, but the body of Christ needs to take responsibility to pray for themselves. We should ask, 'What are you praying? I'll pray in agreement with you.' We are not co-dependent as a church prayer team. We challenge people to pray, so we can pray in agreement with them. We still pray about those things, but we don't need to pray for everything brought to us.

"The greatest shift has been learning to not go ahead into prayer until we have a directive from Holy Spirit. We are learning to hear what God is saying when we pray, then pray in tongues. We pray out loud an interpretation of the tongues as we pray.

"We write down what we are praying for; then when God answers we know it. If there isn't an answer, we go back and ask, 'Did we miss anything? Are we waiting or do we need to pray more or differently?' Nothing is as discouraging as praying faithfully for years and never knowing if God answered. Recording prayer requests and answers has caused a large shift in our prayers. Keeping an accurate record also provides accountability when it comes to the prophetic and words of knowledge.

We need to be seeing answers. Even if it's not the full answer, we know that God is working.

"We understand that not everyone is comfortable with praying out loud. We don't force anyone to pray, but we address fear and release each other. We created a culture where it was okay if it didn't always make sense. If we were wrong, whatever!

"One time, someone came from outside our group and prophesied. She was experienced in prayer and said, 'Your boldness will increase. When you are young and naïve you don't know what you are doing.' Her words were so subtle. She validated people making them feel comfortable, but at the same time undermined them. She wouldn't come under any authority and quoted Scripture so fast that we couldn't keep up. Her Scriptures were inaccurate, however, and she carried a spirit of intimidation. It was ugly!

"A woman in our prayer group had previously been bold to pray out loud. All of a sudden, she stopped. I challenged her, 'You boldly prayed before. You prayed out loud all the time, but since that prophecy, you've stopped.'

"Instantly, I knew in my spirit that something was off, so I brought this new person close to me for a season to keep an eye on her. We don't go looking for problems, but we have to be aware that the enemy would love to come into our prayer meetings to undermine the authority of leadership and what God is doing. We have to guard our prayer community.

"We didn't say anything mean or undermine her in any way but allowed the Holy Spirit to expose what was going on. In the process, we trained the prayer group on how to recognize when opposition enters, repent where they have received something inaccurate, forgive where forgiveness is necessary and move on in prayer.

"We can't afford to allow intimidation to stop us from praying. Neither should we compare our prayer life to others."

Jan experienced corporate prayer as a young child. God trained her in various prayer environments, offering her protection and assistance through the unity of other prayer warriors and intercessors.

"After I accepted the Lord as a child, my mother didn't want to take me to church, but my great-aunt started taking me to the downtown mission when I was eight years old. The prayer room in the mission was my favorite place.

"Before that, my prayer time was with just me and Jesus. By God's design, He brought me into corporate prayer, interceding for the lost and for God to move in revival over our city.

"Corporate prayer broadened my perspective. I began to learn parts of God's heart that I hadn't known before. I began to know Him not only as my best Friend but as someone who desired to use me to cry out for those who needed healing. I prayed with and encouraged others in the mission.

"I saw babies and children sleeping in the pews in the presence of God. I saw women holding tissues wet with their tears as they prayed for wayward sons and daughters. I heard men's voices thunder the Word of God through the room with authority and faith. A base for corporate prayer and intercession was being formed in me.

God heard every cry, even the silent cries.

"As a child, I clearly understood the different expressions of so many people and knew God was receiving it. I knew the prayer room was a good and safe place to be. God was training me. The Lord is the best Teacher.

"I had been praying for my neighbors and their kids to get saved and was able to lead them to the Lord as God began to soften their hearts. I began to see that sometimes prayer takes time. At thirteen years old, I started a little group with all these new Christians from my neighborhood. They weren't religious and didn't know they couldn't pray for big things.

"Again, I saw the way different people prayed. Some were touched by details and circumstances. Others wept for a country when they heard about bombings. Another had the gift of mercy and would pray for the sick. More and more, I began to see God's giftings in people as they prayed.

"I thought, 'God, You need all of us, every single person praying.' "

Though we tend to think of corporate prayer more in a formal setting, taking prayer to the streets is what three women did together on several occasions. Kari and Charlene shared about this different type of corporate prayer synergy.

Kari said,

"I have always loved prayer. As soon as I received Christ, I loved spending time in the Word and praying for people."

Charlene added,

"Three of us women made a couple of trips together: one to Florida, another to Texas. We prayed for every Uber driver we had. There was always one or another of us praying. Kari was so confident.

"This one driver picked us up at the church and asked what was going on. We started telling him about Jesus. Kari asked him if he went to church.

"When I listened to her pray for one man in Texas, every word was filled with truth and boldness. She sat next to the driver who listened intently to what she told him. We didn't feel like we needed to say anything because Kari had it under control. The Word of God comes so naturally to her. Even though he didn't want prayer, she still spoke to him, telling him that there was only one God. Wow! It was awesome!"

Kari said,

"I really felt that he received it. We all had the discernment that he was dabbling in demonic stuff. He wondered what was up or down, right or wrong. That day we gave him answers."

Charlene agreed,

"We knew we had divine connections with our Uber drivers. One was an ex-NBA player who was about seventy years old. We prayed for his knees and his son. We also prayed for a woman at a restaurant who started crying as soon as we hugged her. She was so thankful we prayed. It was pretty amazing how everything worked out."

Kari said,

"When you reach out to who God points you to, they are usually hungry. There was only one person who said, 'I'm good,' when we asked if we could pray for him."

Charlene remembered another encounter,

"My heart went out to a homeless man we gave five dollars to. He tried to run for that money even though he could hardly move, coming as if his life depended on it. I reached out and touched him. There was also a man in Florida we prayed for about a situation with his daughter."

Kari added,

"We just don't know what people are going through. None of those encounters were by accident. God even places people in lineups beside us for a reason. With God, nothing is by chance. Every Uber driver was assigned to us by God. It is fun when we get together. God gets a hold of our hearts and we are obedient to Him. God's Kingdom is inside of each of us. We need to share that Kingdom with those around us. For the people who don't know God yet, they might think we're a little whacked, but when God is on the move, you just do it. Actually, He does it through you."

Charlene agreed,

"Together we spur each other on to pray. I get more boldness with others. It goes both ways, I think. It's good."

Kari added,

"One of the things I'm learning is that religion will say that you have to get all your theology and doctrine right before you can help people. What we are learning is that Jesus said, 'Go!' We don't need to do this school of that or that school of this.

We go with Who is in our hearts, not what is in our heads.

"When we ask for opportunities, we are listening to God and He will open doors and give them to us."

Charlene recounted,

"Heidi Baker says we should get in the prayer closet and then get out of the closet. Get in and get out! Don't stay in the prayer closet—shine out there!"

Kari adds,

"For me, being with other Christians is a huge thing. When you are with others who aren't on fire for God you can lose your passion. It dampens you spiritually. That's not a place I want to be. Being with other believers who pull the best out of you and encourage you is huge. It is vitally important to be with people who are like-minded with you in prayer. Being a Christian doesn't mean we just go to Bible study or join a bless me club."

> *Playing church is a waste of time. We need to get together,*
> *pray and do Kingdom business.*

Clay shared,

"Even in corporate prayer, our personal relationship with God is key. Our hearts have to be right with Him. God looks at the heart, not on the words we utter. God tells us that **The prayer of a righteous person is powerful and effective'** (Jas 5:16).

"Some of the simplest prayers of a new Christian have the greatest faith. At the same time, there is something to be said about maturity, stability and covering. Corporate prayer is any time we worship together and glorify God.

"Corporately, we are called to be like Jeremiah to **'uproot and tear down, to destroy and overthrow, to build and to plant'** (Jer 1:10). We overthrow and destroy in the power of Jesus. We build and plant in its place according to the promises of God. By emptying out one thing, we put something better in its place. Jeremiah gave a great model to follow in our prayers.

"There are different kinds of prayer warriors and intercessors in our prayer meetings. We might think, 'I don't pray that way. That's not going to work.' We have to be accepting of everyone's styles. Some are evangelistic while others do spiritual warfare. Everyone brings something different; together we bring our little piece of the greater picture to fit with someone else's piece. I only see my one little piece, but together we see a whole tapestry of prayer.

"We need to have the grandmothers and grandfathers in the prayer room along with children and the generations between. The young possess an innocence of faith to believe God for anything. The more we age, the less we think we need God and the more set in our ways we can become, thinking prayer has to look a certain way. God is unlimited in what He wants to do corporately through prayer."

Sharon shared a true story from her husband's family.

"When my mother-in-law was carrying my husband's brother, she had to have surgery. The doctors told her that if the baby survived, he would be mentally challenged. There was no hope.

"My father-in-law talked to his father, who immediately called an all-night prayer meeting. I don't know how many attended. The next morning his father phoned back and said, 'Everything is going to be all right.'

"The baby was born healthy and eventually became a university professor.

"That was one night of people giving up sleep to pray with desperation and determination. Are we desperate enough and determined enough to work with God to see Him move and do what only He can do?"

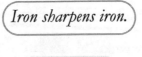

Iron sharpens iron.

Unlocking the Legacy

Corporate prayer occurs anytime two or more people unite in prayer synergy, whether three women on a road trip, twenty-five intercessors each in different locations interceding for a single cause, a church worship gathering, group prayer lines, or any number of other scenarios.

> **"Again, truly I tell you that if two of you on earth
> agree about anything they ask for, it will be done
> for them by my Father in Heaven. For where two or
> three gather in my name, there am I with them."**
> **Matthew 18:19-20**

For an extended season in my early prayer journey, I was physically and spiritually isolated from other intercessors. This verse made me feel even more discouraged. Then I realized that even when I felt alone, I wasn't alone in prayer. Jesus was right there with me. He became the other, the greater, the better Partner in my personal prayer meeting.

Kari and Charlene experienced the benefits of spurring each other on and bringing the best out of each other. Though the writer of Hebrews doesn't mention prayer specifically, the principle is applicable.

> **"And let us consider how we may spur one another
> on toward love and good deeds, not giving up
> meeting together, as some are in the habit of
> doing, but encouraging one another — and all
> the more as you see the Day approaching."**
> **Hebrews 10:24**

I know of no greater encouragement than to gather together in prayer. In fact, prayer is the first habit we see the disciples participate in after Jesus' ascension. He commanded His followers not to leave Jerusalem, but wait for the promised Holy Spirit. They assumed the waiting meant waiting in prayer.

> **"They all joined together
> constantly in prayer. . ."**
> **Acts 1:14**

It doesn't say that anyone grew impatient or left to do other things. They were still together when the promise swooped in on a violent wind and landed with tongues of fire on each of them.

As the days moved forward the fledgling body of believers continued to devote **"themselves to the apostles' teaching and to fellowship, to the breaking of bread and to prayer"** (Acts 2:42). What a solid foundation for any and every body of believers, then and now. Is there any wonder why **"everyone was filled with awe at the many wonders and signs performed by the apostles"** (Acts 2:43)?

Fast forward to the church running into serious problems when their leaders Peter and John were put into prison. Upon their release, where did they go? To the local prayer meeting of course.

> **"Now, Lord, consider their threats and enable your**
> **servants to speak your word with great boldness.**
> **Stretch out your hand to heal and perform signs**
> **and wonders through the name of**
> **your holy servant Jesus."**
> **Acts 4:29-30**

Every decision made in the early church was wrapped in prayer. Every situation they encountered was prayed through (Acts 1:14,24; 2:42). Every new ministry established was birthed out of one prayer group or another (Acts 13:1-3). When Paul wanted to find genuine seekers of God, he scouted out places where people were praying together (Acts 16:11-15). In prison they prayed together until chains fell off, doors opened and doubters became believers (Acts 16:25). Because people were praying in one united effort, an angel masterminded a supernatural jailbreak for Peter (Acts 12:1-18).

The impetus of corporate prayer was Holy Spirit initiated and perpetuated. These apostolic leaders recognized that the synergy of united prayer was the key to unlocking God's vision and legacy for the quickly growing church.

The entirety of unwritten prayer initiatives of the early church will be revealed in Heaven. I wonder where, when and how the enemy shifted prayer into a back room. Why is corporate prayer attended by the few instead of the all within today's churches?

Throughout biblical history when people gathered together,
God moved in supernatural ways.
Enemy armies were decimated;
spiritual territory was taken for God;
hearts were turned back to Him in repentance;
God's presence fell powerfully;
strategies were given;
awe and reverence filled the people.

The Bible is replete with accounts of one-on-one encounters with God but also with significant corporate prayer thrusts. James said that we are not ignorant of the enemy's schemes. One of his greatest ploys is to conquer and divide. Surely that has happened in many prayer circles throughout the ages.

Every revival and spiritual awakening the world has known was birthed by people gathered together on their knees in prayer—even if they numbered two or three. Those revivals launched in prayer grew through continued prayer. In some cases, it was led by children.

> *"A young girl came under conviction and as she prayed,
> she broke down crying, and within five minutes, the
> whole congregation was on their faces crying to God.
> Like lightning and thunder, the power came down,
> transforming a region and bringing tens of thousands to
> conviction, repentance, and salvation in the country."* [1]

The evidence of corporate prayer initiative may be an increase in miracles, signs and wonders. The real substance, however, is in the saving of souls—the ingathering of multitudes into the Kingdom. The miracles capture people's attention to listen to the life-changing message of the Gospel.

God's response to Solomon's prayer at the dedication of the magnificent temple built for His presence declares,

> **"If my people, who are called by my name, will
> humble themselves and pray and seek my face and
> turn from their wicked ways, then I will hear from
> Heaven, and I will forgive their sin and
> will heal their land."**
> **2 Chronicles 7:14**

God, Himself, welcomes us. He calls us, His people
to a position of humility on our knees,
to pray and seek His face,
to desire Him more than His blessings,
to turn from our perverse and wicked ways,
so He can respond to us in unbroken communion together.
Then He will hear, forgive our sins and heal our land. We don't

have to look far to find places where forgiveness and healing are needed. The need for God was great in Solomon's day. How much greater today?

> *"A man by the name of Herman Oster had a barn floor that was under 29 inches of water because of a rising creek. The Bruno, Nebraska, farmer invited a few friends to a barn raising. He needed to move his entire 17,000-pound barn to a new foundation more than 143 feet away. His son, Mike, devised a ladder work of steel tubing, which he nailed, bolted and welded on the inside and the outside of the barn. Hundreds of handles were attached. After a practice lift, 344 volunteers slowly walked the barn up a slight incline. In three minutes, the barn was on its new foundation . . . because they worked together, their strength was multiplied exponentially. If this kind of synergistic power is available in the natural realm, what might the Lord be willing to do for us when we work together spiritually?"* [2]

Taking Territory

"Oh God, my heart cries for You. I long for the day when our prayer meetings will supersede every other gathering of Your people. God, ignite us in prayer. May one prayer meeting flow into another in a never-ending stream of people humbly calling on You and seeking Your face.

" **'LORD I have heard of your fame; I stand in awe of your deeds, LORD. Repeat them in our day, in our time make them known; in wrath remember mercy'** (Hb 3:2). I don't want to just hear about You, I want to see You move again like in the past.

"I ask that Your people would devote themselves again to the apostles' teaching and fellowship, the breaking of bread and prayer, individually and corporately (Acts 2:42).

"It's time, Lord! It's time to declare a **'holy fast; (to) call a sacred assembly. Summon(ing) the elders and all who live in the land to the house of the LORD (our) God, and cry(ing) out to the LORD'** (Jl 1:14).

"Your house shall be a house of prayer once again. Whether it is two or three, or whether it is a dozen, a hundred or more, call us . . . draw us . . . woo us . . . to the place of prayer. May our lives be wholly committed to the mission of prayer. Only prayer produces eternal fruit and undergirds all Kingdom work. O God, we set ourselves to the task.

"Lord, if the house needs to be cleaned, then clean house. I don't ask rashly, but soberly.

"We ask You again to pour out your Spirit on all people. Oh, that our sons and daughters would prophesy, our old men dream dreams, and our young men see visions. Even on Your servants, both men and women pour out Your Spirit in these days' (Jl 2:28-29).

"Thank You, Lord, that already we are seeing prayer initiatives awaken around the world. People of all nationalities, ages and dialects are congregating,

> in homes and churches,
>> under trees and in stadiums,
>>> in prison cells and windowless basements,
>> at any cost, even the risk of their lives,
> for the sole purpose of praying and seeking Your face.

"Ignite an even greater passion for prayer among us. May the synergy of corporate prayer transform entire cities and nations, changing the spiritual landscape globally.

"It is up to us to one by one count the cost and to pay the price to unite in fervent prayer, unlocking legacy and taking territory for the Kingdom of God.

Amen."

> *"From my mother's womb, we attended Wednesday night prayer. For two and a half hours, we knelt in a small church. I will never forget those prayer meetings."*
> — Lois

***

> *"In Bible school, we would pray all day and all night."*
> — June

***

> *"Concerts of prayer, where everyone prays at the same time, are powerful! Corporate prayer made me hungry for personal prayer, and aware of the needs of others."*
> — Jewell

***

Notes

1. Brad Tuttle, *"History Proves that Praying for Revival Matters,"* Charisma News. 2018, https://www.charistmamag.com/spirit/prayer/36194-history-proves-that-praying-for-revival-matters.

2. Dutch Sheets and William Ford III, *History Makers: Your Prayers Have the Power to Heal the Past and Shape the Future* (Ventura, Regal, 2004), 52.

CHAPTER 11

The Help God Sends
– Prayer in Motion

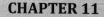

"The only way to have a change is to make a change."
– Kevin [W.]

Leaving the cool dampness of the Asian night, the little group entered the hotel for the last time. With their mission over, they looked forward to a good night's rest before the eighteen-hour flight home—a place far removed from here.

After checking in, I stood waiting by the elevator. A man, hardened by evil, entered with two young girls in tow. The guard who normally stood watch outside promptly escorted the trio to the front desk, bypassing those already waiting in line. The elevator slid open allowing me to enter, leaving the dark presence of the newcomers behind. Suddenly, the guard's hand reached over my shoulder to hold the elevator's doors open. Far from a gracious act for a couple of weary foreigners, he was maintaining ready access to the "merchandise" following.

Moving to the back of the elevator I made room. The two young girls, who lost their right to normal childhood long ago, crowded close pressing themselves against me, not because of a lack of room, but rather out of fear of that man. He entered last but fully occupied half the elevator space.

Sending a silent flare prayer Heavenward, I asked, "Lord, I only have seconds. How can I show your love here?" My heart beat anxiously as I reached out to embrace these two little girls. Their bodies became rigid, instinctively fearing the worst. My heart ached as I felt their steel-like hardness, yet small fragility, close to me. One, then the other, slowly turned and looked into my eyes relaxing as they did so. Smiling tenderly, I gazed unblinking past their eyes into their souls, dark brown pools of lifeless abyss. The armed guard shifted his weight from side to side, fidgeting nervously with his guns while watching me eyefully. Assessing me as an old, harmless intrusion, he relaxed his stance.

The doors opened. They were gone. Led into horrors I dared not imagine.

Did I breathe as the elevator ascended upward to release me to my safe, peaceful room with a lock, absent of violence and cruelty? As I closed the hotel room door behind me, tears of anger mingled with prayers for these two and the millions of others sold in human trafficking. "Why? Who is protecting these defenseless ones? Who but You sees the atrocities they face?" Late into the night, I cried again and again for this and my own nation, woefully self-seeking and willfully blind.

I had prayed about the global blight of human trafficking for many years. I even pledged to surround this team with prayer from my secure spot at home. Now, somehow, here I was with them, ministering in women's shelters, orphanages, a daycare for garbage dump children, picking up street kids, filling their hungry bellies, bathing their bodies and giving them a safe refuge for a few hours. Wherever we went, we shared about a God of deep compassion.

The toll for coming here far surpassed months of preparations, airplane tickets, accommodations, or gifts bringing joy and meeting practical needs. Here where

people are treated like disposable garbage,

eyes are void of life and darkened by horror,

children sleep in trees

so drunken men can't find them,
gods abound, but God, for the most part,
seems hidden—unseen, unknown.

Or is He?

No, we've seen Him. We've heard Him in the laugh of children rescued, fed, loved and protected. We've seen Him in the compassion of the tireless front line workers faithfully serving the least of these. We've felt Him in the selfless giving of those once lost but redeemed by His grace. We've seen Him in the darkness of the nights amongst the brothels. We've witnessed Him in the courage of those walking the path of Hope to a place called Freedom.

God is neither distant nor silent. He is present everywhere. He speaks to those who turn off the din of busyness, willing to hear His still small voice.

Prayer is sanitary, isolated and safe. This is not.

Prayer is good, godly and effective. But it isn't enough.

Prayer is the beginning, the launch to move from the quiet sanctuary of intimate fellowship, into the busyness of the world, getting hands dirty and hearts torn by the brokenness that abounds.

Prayer moves us into prisons and brothels, hospitals and schools. It risks. It loves.

> **". . . faith by itself, if it is not accompanied
> by action, is dead."
> James 2:17**

Prayer immersed in living faith must be active, otherwise, it is clanging, noisy and empty words void of meaning. God calls us into the place of deep intimacy—the bridal chambers of His love. Then He moves us with compassion into the streets and the marketplaces to take that same love to others. So it must be.

Personal Perspectives

Heather shares,

"If I am in both communication with God and community with others, He is able to use all of me. God is unraveling me, making me unable to do anything in prayer that I used to do.

"God recently interrupted me as I was singing, 'It's your breath in my lungs…' He turned it around and started singing those words to me. He said things like, 'You are light in the darkness. You are powerful when you focus your attention on Me.' These kinds of reversals challenge my theology.

"I wish I could tell you that I have exploits where I pray for people and see amazing results. I do pray for healing and am seeing more, but God is showing me that it is the compassion of the Father's heart that matters most.

"I don't want to pray the prayers God can't answer because we're asking Him to do something that He has told *us* to do. The church is meant to be the church. I pray for conviction, 'God there is supposed to be someone involved in this solution. Wake people up! Move the hearts of men.'

"God doesn't wave a wand and make things happen. He is looking for someone to go against the norm, have a voice, and get into action.

"God is challenging me more and more. If I'm willing to pray for God to help a person, am I depleting the strength of my prayer if I'm unwilling to be the solution? If I had five dollars to give, should I pray for God to give someone five dollars? I'm increasingly asking, 'God where are You going to put me in Your Kingdom to see the desires of Your heart fulfilled?'

> *Instead of praying for answers for people,*
> *He wants us to be the answer.*

"I need to be the person willing to manifest all the things Jesus died for. It isn't okay just to pray. Answers come through willing hands, through people's lives and their mouths.

"When I desire others to be healed and whole, I must be willing to roll up my sleeves and get dirty. God says, 'Be My hands and My feet. **'My strength is made perfect in your weakness'** (2 Cor 12:9). God wants us to hear His heart, then get up and be who He is to the world around us. That's prayer!

"I've been praying, 'God, give me the courage to be broken.' When I see the pain in the lives of others, I want to shut down and turn away. I am learning to feel their pain and not push that away. I am not to be broken by it but to bring them Jesus Christ, who is the solution to the earth. Christ in us, reaching the world, is the only hope there is.

"I cannot walk in compassion without feeling enough, being angry enough, fervent enough to go past my "chicken line" to make a difference in the lives of others. God is such a compassionate and loving Father. He has compassion beyond our understanding.

"Until someone has a revelation of the love of God, they will not comprehend it. We can tell them, but it is grasped by revelation. Other people's experience doesn't cut it. We all need to experience God's love for ourselves."

Kari told this story:

"We need to find a church that is going to feed us and equip us to become a blessing to the body of Christ and the world around us. We can't settle for a religious experience.

"When you let God love you, you experience something the world has no concept of. Before we can have horizontal person-to-person relationships, we must first have a vertical *God-with-us* relationship.

"Three of us women went to a healing conference in our city.

During a break, we went to a local restaurant for lunch. I asked the Lord for a word of knowledge for somebody and felt He was saying something about headaches. I often second guess whether I'm hearing God, but a specific waitress seemed to be impressed on my mind.

" 'Is it her?' It seemed like all of a sudden, I was on my feet going toward the counter as if someone was leading me there. I simply asked, 'Do you deal with headaches?'

" 'Oh yes,' she said, 'more than headaches, I get migraines. I'm going through a tough time right now.'

"I could see she was pregnant and she had a large bruise under her eye. I asked if I could pray for her. She was fighting back tears and needed to keep doing her job, so the prayer was brief.

"I said, 'If you give me a piece of paper, I'll write down my name and number. If you need anything, please give me a call. Do you have any family?'

"She did have family, but her boyfriend had kicked her out and she was on her own. Months before, God had instructed one of the other women with us to put a hundred dollar bill in her wallet. She was waiting for God's instructions on what to do with it. When she was paying for her six dollar meal, she felt God prompt her to give the hundred dollar bill to this young waitress. She told her how much God loved her. The rest of us also independently felt God prompt us to tip her generously.

"We never know someone's story. When God directs us to pray or display His love, we need to respond. Even if we aren't sure of what God is saying, it is better to risk than to miss an opportunity.

"This waitress texted me later to thank me. She was so appreciative. Just one little prayer with action blessed her that day and continues to speak to her about God's love."

Lowell shared,

"It is the little things that I look forward to, like asking, 'Holy Spirit, what are You working on this week?' Then I leave it open. Prayer is a living conversation, not just focused on our knees by the bed. Holy Spirit wants to be practical at every moment.

"I was down at the cancer clinic in Mexico for a checkup. There was a lady there who had been given two months to live, but it was two and a half months past that time. She was extremely sick and brought her mother with her. I don't believe they were Christians. Another mother and her daughter seemed to be talking about God. There was also another lady from Texas who was telling us how God had changed her life. The first lady and mother weren't saying anything.

"At some moment the Holy Spirit said, 'Go and pray for her.' We were in a waiting room with others sitting around. It was kind of uncomfortable to go and pray with a stranger, but I asked, 'Is it okay if I pray for you?'

"Really, that prayer time was the best part of my entire trip. She also said it was the best part of her being down there.

> *Being used by God in a real way*
> *is the most rewarding thing on Earth.*

"So much has taken a dim light in my life since so many things are temporary. When those moments come, I'm reminded to take risky steps with Holy Spirit. They may not all work out, but He wants us to reach people in the moment, on any day, with simple things we can do.

"Something I want to become better at is contacting someone once a week, whether that's a Christian or somebody who needs Jesus. When God puts somebody on my heart to pray for, I want to take the next step and say, 'Hey, let's go for lunch.' I'm not an outgoing person, so it's something I have to work at, but so much good comes from those times.

"The Holy Spirit is a gentle teacher."

Charlene says,

"We are praying and shifting as a church from having people come to receive ministry to us going out and finding opportunities. As individuals, God wants us to be actively involved and speak into our community. The concept is fresh and new for us. We are having fun, sharing every success story to keep us encouraged.

"We were looking into a church building situation. God spoke and said, 'You have to wait. I am doing something that is taking you out of the building and into the community.' Even though we were praying and believing for a building, God made it clear that wasn't what He wanted. We don't realize how many things we're praying and believing for that aren't a part of God's plan.

"We have to die to our desires and pray, 'Okay, Lord, what do You want me to do?' "

Betty said,

"Several years ago, I was asked to speak at a women's meeting in Moose Jaw around Mother's Day. I thought it would be easy to tell how God had blessed our family. God gave me a different theme though, about the baptism of the Holy Spirit. I was convicted but still planned to speak on what I originally wanted.

"I took a couple of other women with me. We stopped for a bite to eat, but when I went into the washroom God told me to throw my notes into the garbage. I did!

"I spoke on my theme but brought in the baptism of the Holy Spirit. At the end of the message, I told those who wanted the baptism to go to the other side and speak to the executive while I spoke with those who wanted to receive the Lord. I was committed to praying for salvations.

"I said to God, 'I can't pray for people to receive the baptism.'

> *Who do you think you are?*
> *Of course, you can't! I can!' God said.*

"The first people who came up wanted the baptism. Before I even prayed, they went down in the Holy Spirit and came up speaking in tongues. I thought, 'If it's this easy, okay!' My anointing is primarily for evangelism, but much to my dismay, I realized the baptism of Holy Spirit was also what God was calling me to. It wasn't what I had asked for.

"Praying for others sometimes felt risky. I had seen God do miracles, but thought, 'What if I pray and nothing happens?'

"God said, 'It is none of your business. Your job is to pray! What happens is between me and them.'

"All I have to do is to be a willing vessel. Now that is the way I pray. We have to be willing to change. God is the One who does everything; we can't do anything. I want to be the least of the least."

Mike briefly shared,

"People are searching everywhere, but don't know that God is the answer. We are walking with some friends toward the saving understanding of Jesus. Everything is a mystery to them. The god of this world has darkened their understanding.

"By thinking less about what people think of me, I'm becoming increasingly bold to pray for people, even strangers. Now it seems more natural. I believe God can make a difference in people's lives. I know what He has already done and the power He has.

"Reaching out to people in practical ways and praying for them is generally received well. Many people are grateful. I don't need to understand why God wants things done a certain way.

> *Understanding is not the prerequisite for obedience.*

"The Holy Spirit is the One who does the work."

Mark said,

"Though I have been involved in the lives of younger men for many years, I have reached the point where I refuse to mentor anyone who is not actively evangelizing, discipling and praying for others. I try to follow Paul's advice to Timothy to train up those who are investing in others (2 Tm 2:2).

"God's power is at work. These young men are doing the real deal. They're helping in their local church and are also out on the streets ministering to anyone God points them to regardless of their religious affiliation. Sharing the Gospel first by ministering to practical needs opens the door wider to speak about Jesus.

"Many people are being healed. Many are also coming to faith in Jesus Christ as a result. Jesus is alive! He is waiting for someone willing to be His hands, feet, and mouthpiece.

"I would love to see whole families doing this together. The Holy Spirit works through people of all ages.

> *Jesus is the Healer. It isn't about us, but Him!*

"When you discover how faithful God is, you can't help but want to share Him with others. God desires to bring spiritual freedom and healing to everyone. I'm asking God to speak to me and to open my ears to hear clearly while petitioning Him for people's hearts and the freedom He wants to bring to them. God has given me an awareness of the physical and spiritual needs He wants to meet right here in my city.

"I don't want this legacy to stop with me. It's important to be intentional about encouraging others to step out, take the risk and follow whatever God is leading them to do. I want them to challenge others to do the same. When we listen to God's prompts and obey, we will see more of what God can and will do.

> *Prayer creates a sensitivity to others and confidence to share God's love with those who need it.*

Patrick believes we need to take bigger risks in praying for others.

"I was praying for people to be healed, stretching out and taking risks in prayer. When I went on a Global Mission trip, I began to see things happen when I prayed for people.

"Now I pray for healing and various things with an extreme amount of faith. I'm confident that prayers are going to be answered.

"I pray for words of knowledge before I enter a church or a time of ministry. Sometimes days before, I will receive a word and people will be touched by God and healed. Often God will give me a word of knowledge through feeling pain but knowing it's for someone else. It's extremely subtle but I have peace in knowing. I have to press in and take the risk even before I have the confidence that the Lord is speaking to me. Other times, it's been clear and I'm able to be confident and direct with a word.

"I had a word of knowledge for a hernia. As the person stood up, it disappeared right then. The lady felt it change and heal. It just tickles me when God uses me that way.

> *God shows up when you are willing to take a risk.*

"When we are pressing into God, striving for His excellence and goodness, wanting to see Him glorified on earth, He shows up. It isn't about us, but rather about what Holy Spirit wants to do. We don't get attached to the word God gives us.

"I stood in the ministry team line at the altar and gave the name of a lady, "Marlaina." No one stood up. I figured I missed it. Later a lady approached one of our team members and said, 'I am Marlaina. I think that word was for me.' My team mate asked what she needed prayer for and she said her stomach. When the team member put her hand on the lady's stomach and prayed for healing, there was movement underneath, like a demonic presence. The lady was totally healed; I was elated. I hadn't missed it!

"We need to stay humble. Holy Spirit has things under control. He wants us to be willing to take the risk and He will use us. It's about Him and the person receiving, not about us."

> *If you are not aware of God for yourself, you aren't going to be aware of the needs of others.*

Keith says,

"Prayer is an uplifting time. I bring God the burdens of others so I don't carry them anymore. The weight shifts from me to Him. I leave it at the foot of the cross knowing the rest is up to God. That's not to say I don't pray again. Sometimes prayer takes a while. I believe we aren't supposed to quit praying until we see an answer.

"Even as I am praying for other men, I maintain a relationship with them. Whenever I encounter them, I ask God what I can say to spur them on.

> *We are playing a part in the answer to our prayers coming into fruition by making ourselves available.*

"I know that it doesn't stop at prayer. We leave it in God's hands but say, 'Use me where You want.' If there is still something God wants me to do, yes! We can be instrumental in the answers to prayer by allowing ourselves to be used by God.

"One afternoon some people came to the door needing money. I felt strongly that I was supposed to help them, so I filled their tank with fuel and gave them cash to help them out. A lot of times, I pay for someone's meal. I'm cautious but when God wants to use me, I want to be available. I believe God wants us to be the hands and feet to our prayers."

For Allison, combining prayer with action, in various capacities, has always gone hand in hand as a part of her Christian walk.

"I came to know the Lord in an outward-focused church. The weekend after I was saved, I was doing door to door evangelism. To me, that was normal. Because of that beginning, prayer and action have gone together.

"A few years ago, I came to a place of surrendering to God and trusting Him to provide for me. I was wrestling and praying about giving up my regular income. I realized that the monks, nuns and others who swear a vow of poverty are perhaps closer to the heart of Jesus than we fully understand.

"Covenanting with God to give everything I have for Him and never turning anyone away who has a need sounds far more like Jesus than hoarding and seeking personal prosperity for myself and my family. I don't think that's a poverty mentality, but rather a generous spirit—willing to sacrificially give to others as a witness for Christ.

Faith-filled prayer includes trusting God to meet my every need and a generous spirit to trust Him as I give to others.

"God burdened me to pray for Central Asia in 2010. In a dream in 2016, I knew God was telling me to go to a specific nation in that region, but it wasn't until 2019 that I actually went. Through those years, a lot of prayer went into that nation and peoples. By faith I prepared to go, but before I booked my ticket I needed someone who would host me. Last summer, a missionary family invited me to come and stay with them.

"While I was there, I had a vivid prophetic dream in which there was an intense battle going on for the soul of someone. When I woke up, I continued to intercede for that person.

"That day my host invited me along on a camping trip with

several other female missionaries from nine different nations and agencies. One of the local missionary women had spent a lot of time with a Muslim friend from a neighboring country and brought her along. This Muslim woman was fasting for Ramadan. I was able to connect with her because I had spent time in other Muslim communities breaking fast with Muslim families.

"The Holy Spirit gave me the revelation that this was the Muslim woman I had dreamed about. She was starting to seek Christ and was experiencing an intense battle for her soul. I shared my dream with my host so we could be praying for her together.

"When we went into a high-altitude camp, we experienced altitude sickness. The weather was cold and snowy; we all felt like we were freezing. We made a campfire to heat our supper, but she stayed in her tent while we were eating. Afterward, we started to sing songs. I remembered that in the dream, I sang a song in Russian. This Muslim woman's first language happened to be Russian, so I sang the song from my dream. Nothing apparent happened.

"She ended up breaking her fast. Originally, she had planned to go to Turkey to study. Soon after our camping trip, however, she started working full time for this Christian non-profit organization staffed by missionaries. She also started reading the Bible with one of her friends.

"My part was a drop in the bucket compared to the relational investment of others directly involved in her life. However, I believe that my prayers and obedience were a small part of her breakthrough and coming nearer to the Lord. She is still reading the Bible and is close to accepting Christ."

Unlocking the Legacy

When God wants to send help, be the help God sends!

> **"After this the Lord appointed seventy-two
> others and *sent them* two by two ahead of him
> to every town and place where he was about
> to go. He told them, 'The harvest is plentiful,
> but the workers are few. *Ask the Lord* of the
> harvest, therefore, to send out workers into
> his harvest field. *Go!* I am *sending you* out
> like lambs among wolves."**
> **Luke 10:1-3**
> **(Emphasis mine)**

I inwardly laugh every time I read this passage. Jesus instructs His followers to pray for more people actively working for His kingdom. Then He immediately says, "Go! You're it! You didn't know, but the one you were praying for is you." How often have I thought I was praying

   for a good cause somewhere else,

     for someone better equipped to take the lead,

       for somebody unknown to fill the gap,

     for other people to catch the wave of God's intent,

  for the anonymous whosoever to leap into action,

when God was saying to me, "Go! Yes, you—piously kneeling, tearfully interceding—get up and go!" Why is it easy to pray for some unknown anyone to do what I am unwilling to get involved in? Immaturity, apathy, indifference? It isn't just the Pharisees of Jesus' day who didn't want to get

   their hands dirty

     or their theology realigned,

       their routine uncomfortably shifted

     or their reputation put at risk,

  their resources stretched

     or their neat schedules disturbed.

We too can become self-righteous in our faith and immobilized from action. Pray? Yes! Wait for God's direction? Absolutely! But then, step out, take the risk, and touch the lives of those for whom we are praying. Reaching out to people in practical ways can feel intimidating.

If we are serious about unlocking the legacy God has for our generation, movement is required on our part. Words are good, but work gets the job done.

James spoke honestly,

> **"What good is it, my brothers and sisters, if some-
> one claims to have faith but has no deeds? Can
> such faith save them? Suppose a brother or a sister
> is without clothes and daily food. If one of you
> says to them, 'Go in peace; keep warm and well
> fed,' but does nothing about their physical needs,
> what good is it? In the same way,** *faith by itself*, **if it
> is not accompanied by action, is** *dead*.**"**
> **James 2:14-17**
> **(Emphasis mine)**

"Active faith believes God to the point of action." [1]

Prayers of faith are essential in unlocking the legacy God wants to be released, but powerless if unaccompanied by actions. God calls our prayer efforts *"dead"* unless we move from the prayer room to the workroom.

As the testimonies of these express, God responds to our obedience. When we choose to do things God's way, in His timing, it releases Him to do what He desires in and for the people around us.

Mike reminded us that we don't have to understand why God wants things done a certain way before obedience takes action. The combination of faith plus obedience opens the way for God to move.

When God speaks to willing servants, the Word He speaks is activated supernaturally into lives. God makes able those who are available. When our hearts partner with God's great compassion, His love explodes onto the scene in tangible ways, bringing healing and redemption.

*"Whoever wants to be the works of
Jesus must pray in His Name.
Whoever prays in His Name
must work in His Name."* [2]

When God asks us to do or say something, our actions and

words affect both the natural and spiritual realm. Like Patrick expressed, that should tickle us!

Matthew's Gospel speaks about Jesus spending time early in the morning praying, then getting up and moving throughout the area teaching and doing. He commanded His disciples to do the same. Pray first; then go!

> "*Jesus went* through all the towns and villages, *teach-ing* in their synagogues, *proclaiming* the good news of the kingdom and *healing* every disease and sick-ness. When he saw the crowds, he had compassion on them, because they were harassed and helpless, like sheep without a shepherd. Then he said to his disciples, 'The harvest is plentiful but the workers are few. Ask the Lord of the harvest, therefore, to *send out* workers into his harvest field."
> **Matthew 9:35-38**
> **(Emphasis Mine)**

In the lives of the early apostles, the combination of prayer activated through deeds resulted in the exponential expansion of the church. Their actions created a willingness amongst the people to listen to their message. As the practical needs of people were met,

> "So the word of God spread. The number of disciples in Jerusalem increased rapidly and . . . became obedient to the faith."
> **Acts 6:7**

The key to unlocking the legacy was and is prayer in action! God hasn't changed our mandate or His methods of reaching the lost and strengthening believers.

> "*God has called us to be His answer to the world's troubles, not to run from them.*"[3]

Taking Territory

"Oh God, I come before You ashamed—ashamed of my clean hands, my guarded heart, my sterile prayers. Forgive me. For too long I have looked at the world from my safe and religious position. Forgive me. I have been too comfortable with Your many blessings and too enamored by Your presence to go to those You love. Forgive me.

"Lord, I desire a risky faith; a faith that shakes me from apathy and indifference; a faith that jolts me from complacent religious practice.

" **'Send out workers into the harvest fields;'** the fields are ripe and ready (Mt 9:38). Start with me! Give me Your compassion
> that shakes off fatigue and moves me to action,
> > that creates generosity to share with others,
> > > that risks being returned evil for good,
> that sacrifices so others may have,
> > that breaks so the broken will be mended,
> > > that touches with love the unlovable.

"When my life is over, I want to say with Paul, **'I have fought the good fight, I have finished the race, I have kept the faith'** (2 Tm 4:7). I want to meet You with nothing left in the bag of resources You have given me, leaving no Kingdom assignment undone.

"Unlocking legacy means giving the living water of Your Spirit to the thirsty and the fresh manna of Your Word to the hungry. Fill me with a generosity that lavishly pours out all You have given me. With You, there is no lack! In You, there is no shortage!

"All I have is Yours. All I am is for Your Kingdom service. **'Here I am! Send me!'** (Is 6:8). Send me where You desire; lead me where You want me to go. I hold nothing back. I have become a radical lover of the Lord Jesus Christ. I am not my own. O Lord, may I not miss the opportunity to be
> Your hands of service,
> > Your heart of love,
> > > Your means of provision,
> > > > Your voice of encouragement, or
> > > > > Your arm of support.

"Only when I am continually poured out, can You then constantly fill me. I'm not a reservoir for Your blessings, but a channel of

Your goodness and grace. Easy in! Easy out! Fill me and empty me for the sake of Your Name, O Lord.

"Release and unlock Your legacy through prayer-filled action.

Amen."

> *"We are to be the answer to prayer by one act*
> *of obedience at a time." – Heather*

***

> *"I am always open and listening to Holy Spirit,*
> *wanting to respond in obedience to Him—whatever way He*
> *wants, any place at any time." – Kate*

***

> *"God is looking. Am I willing to be the one standing in the*
> *gap? Am I willing to be led by God?" – Clay*

***

Notes

1. Kathryn Kuhlman, *I Believe in Miracles: Streams of Healing from the Heart of a Woman of Faith*, rev.upd., (Gainesville, Bridge-Logos Publishers, 2001), 55.

2. Andrew Murray, *With Christ in the School of Prayer* (Springdale, Whitaker House, 1981), 140.

3. Bill Johnson and Kris Vallotton, *The Supernatural Ways of Royalty: Discovering Your Rights and Privileges of Being a Son or Daughter of God* (Shippensburg: Destiny Image Publishers, 2006), 180.

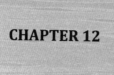

CHAPTER 12

The Power of Testimony – Do It Again, Lord!

> *"Prayer does not equip us for the greater work;*
> *prayer is the greater work."*
> *— Author Unknown*

The prayer principles within this book are tangible and potent only because they are based on the inerrant Word of God. Everything about prayer originates from and rests securely upon the foundation of God—His divine character and faithfulness: God drawing us to Himself in a personal relationship; God turning His ear toward our faint cries and warring shouts; God empowering us to move with His power and through His authority.

The Bible describes faith as **"the substance of things hoped for, the evidence of things not seen"** (Heb 11:1 KJV). The evidence of God moving through His miraculous power in answer to prayer could not be expounded in a few simple writings. However, this closing chapter includes mini-testimonies of prayer rooted in faith, becoming substance.

Joy-Lyn could write her own book on the miracles she has witnessed God do in answer to prayer, but here are just a few:

"I was in the chemistry laboratory completing an experiment when I received a word of knowledge for the girl sitting across from me in the lab. I felt she was having a problem with the right side of her neck or shoulder, perhaps from a sports injury or gymnastics.

"When we were finished our work, I asked her about it. She did have an injury, but it was from softball. She was experiencing tension and pain on the side of her neck, running down into her shoulder. We prayed right there in the chemistry lab at the university. God touched her. She almost started crying and said, 'That made my day!'

***

"A couple of years ago, my Mom and I went to a garage sale in a little church across the street from our house. I thought I had a word of knowledge for one lady about her knee. 'No,' she said, 'but my shoulder is in a lot of pain.'

"I asked if I could pray for her. 'Sure,' she said, 'but I'm going to keep shopping.' After praying, I asked her to test it out. Before prayer, she could only raise her arm parallel to the floor, but now she could raise it a little higher, although it still hurt.

"I asked if I could pray again, 'Okay,' she said, 'I'm shopping, but go for it.' I prayed again and asked her to check it a second time. She lifted her arm all the way up and gasped, 'Who . . . are . . . you?' as she backed up.

" 'It's Jesus! It is *all* Jesus!' I said.

"She turned around and quickly left. I walked away laughing and thought, 'We're in a church. I don't know what you expected.'

It goes to show that healing isn't as normal as it should be.

***

"After my first year of university, I needed a job and applied to several places but didn't receive any response. I started praying about it.

"I already knew that tithing was not an option but an important biblical principle. I had tithed before but wasn't diligently keeping track of every source of income. Up until then, I hadn't made tithing a priority in my spiritual walk.

"After I prayed for a job, the Lord quickly and clearly said, 'You start tithing and I'll give you a job.'

"That was on a Tuesday. Immediately, I took the time to figure out, as far back as I could remember, what I hadn't tithed from and tithed on that income. By Friday, I was offered a job.

"I received a random phone call for an employment opportunity that I hadn't even applied for stating, 'We think you would be good for this position.' That was probably the quickest answer to prayer I've ever received.

"As soon as I obeyed, God provided!

***

"At work, I was picking up a couple of kids from visiting their mother. When she helped put the kids into the car, I asked if she experienced headaches. After confirming it, we prayed together. Immediately, she felt a lot better. The Muslim girl I was working with that day got to hear the prayer and see this woman's healing. Then I invited the woman to come to church with me.

" 'Sure,' she said, 'I'd like that.'

" 'Great! I'll pick you up tonight.'

211

"That evening I went to the women's shelter to pick her up and waited for twenty minutes but she never came to meet me. I was about to leave when another lady walked in with crutches. We started talking and I felt led to pray for her. She was in a lot of pain and had been on crutches for ten years because of a failed surgery. After I prayed, she tested it out. It was somewhat better but not completely, so we prayed again.

"She ended up walking pain-free without her crutches and then gave her heart to Jesus. Another lady, who had come into the lobby, heard the prayer, saw the miracle and began thanking God."

> *It is really cool when God shows up at work!*

Even though Joy-Lyn wasn't completely accurate with the words of knowledge, when she stepped out in faith, trusting God, He graciously healed those around her.

BreAnn shared,

"I haven't always felt comfortable praying for others but as I learned to trust the Holy Spirit, I became more willing to pray.

"I have seen several significant answers to prayer. My whole family started praying for my uncle when the doctors believed he had a tumor in his neck. Surgery was performed, but they found it was actually a lymph node, not cancer, and it was resolved. Praise the Lord! That was my earliest loud answer to prayer.

"For several years, I was struggling with knee pain and had to go down the stairs one at a time. When a young girl prayed for me at a youth retreat, I felt something hot in my knee. That ongoing knee pain hasn't returned. Now, I can walk down the stairs normally.

"Our child is one hundred percent a miracle and an answer to prayer. My husband and I were told we would never be able to have children on our own. We both felt no urgency to look into in vitro fertilization or adoption. God gave us a great deal of peace to continue praying and waiting on Him. We became pregnant by the hand of God within three months. Our child is nothing short of a miracle!

"I realize that not everyone's prayers get answered like that even though they are far more faithful than we are. God hears every prayer. Not a sparrow falls to the ground without God seeing and knowing (Mt 10:29). Sometimes our desires are fulfilled before our eyes, at other times 'no' or 'wait' is an answer.

> *We say with confidence that our prayers are answered because we know who we are praying to.*

"We have a God who cares deeply for us. Sometimes the tangible answer we experience is God's peace during imperfect circumstances. We may never understand how God chooses to answer our prayers."

Emmanuel actively pursues spiritual gifts. The list of miracles he has witnessed in his young life spans far.

"I keep pressing in to see God move miraculously in the lives of others. I don't create doctrines based on my lack of understanding, however.

"For years I prayed for people with one leg shorter than the other to be healed without seeing results. Nothing! Even though I was frustrated, I knew that God wasn't the issue, but

I was. Then I asked a friend who often sees healing in this area to pray for me. The very first person I prayed for after that was healed. Now at least ninety percent of those I pray for with that condition are healed.

"If the door hasn't been opened to me, I knock again. Then, I keep on knocking (Mt 7:7-8). For me, to pray without ceasing means to not give up (1Thes 5:17).

"There was a fellow in serious condition in the hospital. I don't think I have fought for someone's life so much in prayer. I kept in touch with his mother and knew he was getting worse instead of better. The doctors gave him no hope of recovery. He was in a coma and given twenty-four to forty-eight hours to live. I, and many others, kept pushing through in prayer. Not only did he recover, but he gave his life to the Lord. He's alive and well today.

"That is a recent example of praying for someone without immediate results. It doesn't mean we pray 24-7, but we pray without giving up. Although we should all make intentional time for prayer, that should not be the *only* time we pray.

> *God is a Good Father.*
> *He doesn't inflict pain to teach us a lesson.*
> *That would be abusive! God is so gracious and wonderful.*

"Even though I have seen many others healed, I have rarely been healed of anything. My theology is that God always desires to heal. He takes ugly situations and transforms them into something beautiful.

"We need to be deeply grounded in the Word of God; otherwise, we will lower God to meet our pain. If we anchor ourselves in the Word, we won't diminish God in any way. I'm okay with not understanding why God sometimes heals and doesn't at other times. Even though I don't understand, I keep pressing in to see and know Him more."

Caleb shared,

"Prayer is a two-way conversation involving both talking to God and listening for Him to speak. Even in insignificant things, I ask God for help.

"Not that long ago, I lost my wallet. After coming home from a restaurant, I couldn't find it anywhere. After looking everywhere to no avail, I prayed, asking God to put it in a place where I could see it. A little while later, I noticed it on the living room couch, clearly visible.

> *There is no supernatural lifestyle without prayer.*

"When I was in Grade 12 my marks weren't amazing. I wanted to find a job so I could buy a car. I didn't plead or demand, but simply prayed only once, 'Jesus, if You want me to have a car You're going to have to give me one.' I didn't tell anyone that I prayed. Shortly after, a former pastor called and offered me a car. Was that a coincidence? I don't think so. When we allow the Holy Spirit into our lives and conversations, we will see things happen."

Sometimes, just hearing God's voice is the greatest miracle, as Karen discovered.

"A little while ago, God unusually demonstrated His love to me, thereby increasing my faith.

"My husband and I were driving to the city on a beautiful, sunny fall day. All was quiet and the view picturesque. With my husband behind the wheel, I silently enjoyed the ride, gazing blissfully out the window of the car at the splendid fall colors. Amongst the other trees, a smaller brightly colored red tree seemed to stand out, catching my attention and filling me with awe.

" 'Wow!' I said to myself, 'Do I ever like that tree! It's gorgeous!'

" 'Thank you,' I heard, 'I like that one too. It's one of my favorites.' The voice came so quickly and unexpectedly, I was surprised. Did I hear right? Yet, I knew beyond a doubt that it was not my own thoughts.

"For days I marveled at what had happened. It made me feel oddly special—like a secret shared between two people who love each other. I wanted to share it with others, but I knew that it wouldn't mean the same to them as it did to me.

"Since then I've wondered why He would speak to me about something so insignificant. How many times had I begged and longed for a word from God, without hearing anything? Now, out of the blue, when I wasn't even praying, He spoke so clearly to me."

Jewell experienced healing of an arm injury.

"I had a bad accident and received a "dinner fork" fracture to my wrist. I was in a cast for a long time and had also gone through many painful procedures trying to get it to release. Nothing helped. Because it hadn't healed properly, I had limited use of my hand.

"While working at a summer camp, all the counselors gathered around me to pray after their morning meeting. Most of them knew I had received a spinal injury and broken ribs from a serious accident. Because they loved me, they wept as they prayed over me. Everyone, except for one fellow, prayed for my spine and the pain I was enduring. He prayed for my wrist and arm.

"I had been seated on a chair encircled by all these young people. When they finished praying, there was a complete circle of tears shining on the floor around me. They asked if I felt any different. Though I was encouraged by their prayers and felt so blessed by their love, I didn't feel any change physically.

"I continued the day, performing my duties as best I could. Later in the evening, since there was usually someone who needed a nurse's attention after the games time, I was sitting by the medical cabinet waiting. While I was waiting, I went to flex my arm to stretch it.

"I was shocked! For the first time in a year, my wrist had full flexibility in both directions. I suddenly realized my wrist was completely healed. It hasn't bothered me since.

> *In God's perfect time, it only took a minute.*

"That year, there were several other healings that occurred at camp including a girl who had experienced multiple concussions. It was an exciting time for the campers to witness God perform physical healings."

Christie shared a miracle of provision.

"I had applied to enroll in a university program but was reluctant to take out any student loans. I said to God, 'I'm not spending money on this program. If I'm going back to school it has to be paid for.'

"I was informed that I would need to retake an exam to qualify for the program. Because of my schedule, I didn't have time to study. I asked several people to pray for me as I rewrote the exam and for the finances for the program.

"The way things worked out, the administrators didn't care about my grade score on the exam. They also decided that they would cover the cost of the program, plus my rent and utilities. School is very expensive, so it was a big deal to have all my expenses covered. I saw the provision of the Lord as He gave me everything I needed."

Visions, both her own and others, have impacted Yogeswari's life resulting in miracles.

"When my husband lost his job, our daughter was six years old. We decided not to have any more children because, in India, there are no child benefits. Parents have to pay for everything including all medical and educational expenses from kinder-garten through university. Without my husband working, we couldn't afford another child.

"My pastor's wife had a vision. 'God is trying to give you some-thing and you're abandoning it. That's why your husband has lost his job.'

" 'What? How could my husband's losing his job be related to me not planning on having any more children?'

"She said, 'Don't ask questions. Tell God that you will let your son be conceived and that you will have this child. Then there won't be any further problems with him finding a job. Please promise God that you will receive the child He wants to give to you.'

"That's what I did. Our son is a promise. Not that we didn't face problems, but my husband immediately found a very good job. When our first child was born, we had to pay for everything. With our son, my husband's employer paid for everything including a cesarean section. God gave us a son and paid every expense.

"When I was pregnant, I prayed, 'The son of David is going to come to me. I want Solomon's wisdom for this child.'

"A while later, a pastor prophesied over our son, 'You are a son of promise. You are having David's promise in you.' That pastor confirmed it, even though it was something only my husband and I knew. I know my son will be a person of praise and prayer just like David was. Our son knows he is a child of promise."

God answered Kristina's lifelong prayer in several ways.

"My maternal grandmother was Ukrainian Catholic. Maybe she knew the Lord, but I didn't know for sure. As a little girl, I always tried to share the Lord with her. In her late eighties, when I was in Bible college, she was in a nursing home and started having heart problems.

"I was concerned. I tried to share the Lord so many times with her. She was either hard of hearing or had selective hearing. I'm not sure which! One day after visiting her in the nursing home, I walked back to our house and was almost home when the Lord said, 'Go back and tell her about Me.'

"I was so mad, 'I have told her so many times about You.'

"I tromped back to the nursing home, went into my grandmother's room and sat on her bed. It wasn't even close to a heartfelt explanation of the Gospel. 'Grandma, you are a sinner. We're all sinners. Jesus died on the cross for you. He rose again. You need to ask Him into your heart. Do you want to do that?'

"She said, 'Yes.'

"I was kind of dumbfounded and hardly knew what to do but led her through the sinner's prayer and left.

"My grandmother had struggled with anxiety throughout her lifetime. Because of the heart problems she was having, I prayed, 'Okay God, she has received You. Please don't let her struggle with fear and depression right now. Please, can we see some tangible results of You in her life.'

"The first of three answers to my prayers was that she came to know Jesus.

"Second, my grandmother's new-found passion was playing bingo. She loved playing bingo and would give the quarters she had won to the visiting grandchild of the moment. My Mom called me up one day when I was back in Bible school to tell me that my grandmother passed away. To me, an answer to prayer is that my grandmother, who wrestled with fear, died doing the thing she loved—playing bingo. Furthermore, she had just won her second game; they put the money in her hand; she smiled, hung her head and went home to be with the Lord. There was no pain or fear in this new Christian lady.

"The third answer was that the Catholic priest from grandmother's town was too busy to do her prayers and we were able to have our little Baptist church pastor who knew and visited her in the nursing home, come to do the prayers. All of my mom's siblings, nieces and nephews came. At my grandmother's prayers, my family, who didn't know the Lord, heard the Gospel being shared by our Baptist pastor.

"My grandmother appeared to be hard of hearing, but this pastor said at my grandmother's little service, 'I visited Mary many times and shared the Lord with her. Recently, I asked her, "Do you want to receive the Lord?"' '

"She said, 'Kristina and I already dealt with that.'

"Somehow through my obligatory actions, 'Okay God, I'll go share with my grandmother,' she got it. Through whatever hearing matters were happening, she understood. God answered my very special lifelong prayer in several ways."

Prayer wasn't a daily practice when Keith prayed for his wife.

"My wife experienced hip pain constantly. It was uncertain the direct cause but no doubt a heavy physical workload was a contributing factor—handling hundred-pound grain bags, flipping and rolling out hay bales by hand, gardening and a multitude of other strenuous tasks.

"Her father had undergone both shoulder and hip replacement surgery. The enemy taunted her, that she would soon end up the same way. Each night she would crawl into bed struggling to find a comfortable position to sleep.

"We can't remember whose idea it was, mine or hers, but someone decided it was time for prayer. I laid my hand on her hip not knowing how to even pray. Before I could say a word, I felt an intense heat flowing through my hand. She felt nothing but peacefully went to sleep.

"The next morning, she woke up completely healed. She never experienced any pain or discomfort in her hip again. God did it. He answered my silent prayer and it only took a minute."

The Love Bus is an inner-city ministry bringing food and necessities to prostitutes and gang members. I don't join this dedicated group of volunteers often, but each time I do, I learn as much from the street people as from the workers.

"I arrived early to help prepare the sandwiches and fruit that we would be taking along with us. We had a brief time of prayer and received final instructions before heading out for the night. We were told not to let the neighborhood children, who would be the first to bombard the bus, take all the food before we reached the streets.

"Sure enough, while we were loading the bus, children started clambering up the steps looking for food to take home with them. It wasn't long before I began to resent their demands. We gave each child a drink of hot chocolate and a supply of food before escorting them back off the bus.

"I honestly had to go and sit at the back of the bus for a few minutes just to repent of my nasty attitude. It was obvious these children didn't have much to call their own; critical judgment had no place in God's work.

"Soon the bus was rolling through the core area of our city, stopping to welcome anyone onto the bus for a warm cup of coffee, hot chocolate or something to eat. The Love Bus offers protection, safety, love and dignity to everyone.

"Several hours later, a man and woman entered. Age is hard to determine on the streets; it isn't measured by years, but rather by experience. The trauma of inner-city life distorts and molds people leaving little room for normalcy. Before leaving the bus, they both received prayer, hugs as warm as the coffee, and love enough to carry them through the night. They stood outside chatting with the driver for a while.

"Soon the driver re-entered asking if we could change our route and head outside the normal area to give this couple a ride. We all agreed. Back on the bus, they came.

"I slipped over beside the woman, beginning a conversation. She had been in the hospital because she had shot up with a deadly cocktail of substances. Within hours, they quickly released her to fend for herself. Her legs were still grossly swollen from the effect of the self-inflicted potion.

" 'They feel like shattered fiberglass hockey sticks—each splinter tearing at me with terrible pain.' she explained.

"At that moment, I forgot that she was a drug addict, heading to get another fix. My heart reached out before my hand touched her leg, as I asked, 'May I pray for you?'

"Together we prayed for the swelling to dissipate and the pain to be removed from her body. I asked her to test her legs and see if there was any change. She stood on them for a moment before sitting back down, 'Yes, they're a little better.'

"I explained that God is so big and loving that He doesn't want to make things just a little better but bring complete healing. She agreed to allow me to pray again, before testing her legs a second time. Now they were almost completely better and the swelling had gone down considerably. One more time we prayed.

"This time when she checked her legs, they were completely pain-free. For the first time that night, a giant smile spread across her face, deepening the wrinkles on her cheeks and exposing blackened teeth. Joy and unbelief mingled with gratitude, 'God did it! He took my pain!'

> *God showed up on the most dangerous streets in the most dangerous city in our nation. How awesome is that!*

"Soon we were at their desired destination. Again, I moved to the back of the bus for a time of solitude. Tears of gratitude oozed from my heart down my cheeks. Never before had I witnessed God's love so tangibly as on the night He healed a little prostitute and drug addict. The greatness of His love and goodness stretched beyond my ugly attitudes and her destructive habits, exposing itself to a world gone mad."

Fortunately, God's desire to intervene in people's lives is far greater than our handicaps and hang-ups. Prayer's effectiveness is never dependent on our ability, but rather on God's availability to move.

Helen shares her personal experience.

"We get to be co-laborers with Christ. How exciting is that? He shows me something and I get to pray with Him. We may think we should pray for someone, but real prayer is God moving on us to pray. I need to be hearing what Holy Spirit is saying so I can be more effective.

"Having said that, I remember being at a training on prayer but was sicker than a dog that night. I was paired up with a girl who had a bad foot. Honestly, I couldn't have cared less about her foot. I just wanted to go home. I felt as dry as toast, prayed for her foot and she was healed.

"I thought, 'God, You are good.' I didn't care less. She was ecstatic!

"Someone said to me later, 'You must have felt elated?'

"I said, 'No! I was shocked.'

"I really didn't want to be there and didn't want to be praying. The answers don't depend on us. God is so anxious to answer prayer He will use anybody He can find. We are not always in the right mood. Sometimes we don't feel like we're connected to God at all. We don't have to sense Him or feel Him. He is the One who does it!

"I would like more faith in prayer to ask bigger and not limit God. He is beyond what we could think or imagine."

I've had my own dry as toast experiences.

"A couple of years ago, I had been to a discipleship class and was hurrying to pick up groceries before the store closed. I was overtired and anxious to start the hour trek home. Even though the class should have given me a more godly attitude, I think I forgot the Christian part of me behind when I left the building.

"The icy Arctic wind swept across the parking lot, blasting its cold onslaught against anyone brave enough to be outside. As I reached the door of the grocery store, a woman and small child approached, asking for money. Because panhandlers often frequent this spot, I had grown suspicious of their stories and motives.

"Annoyed I invited them inside the doorway, selfishly wanting to escape the chill myself. She explained how they traveled across the country when her husband was offered a job here. However, by the time they arrived, the position had already been filled.

"The whole family—father, mother and five children—were now living in their van. They had no food or money to provide for the essentials. Her story neither impressed nor convinced me. I sized them both up—a desperate woman and her young daughter, perhaps five years old.

"Welcoming her to pick up a couple of baskets to fill with groceries, I told her that I didn't have money, but would buy them enough food for a meal. We went through the fresh produce picking up groceries. She cautiously began filling her basket, asking for permission for each item she chose.

"Halfway through the produce aisle, she talked about having a bad headache. My attitude was so crappy, I thought, 'If you are taking advantage of me, the least you can do is let me pray for you.' Thankfully my words didn't match my thoughts that night, so I expressed it more like, 'I believe in Jesus Christ and I have seen Him heal many times. May I pray for you?'

225

"The woman was dressed in Middle Eastern garments, so I'm not sure what her religious beliefs were. She was so desperate, however, that she agreed to let me pray.

"Honestly, the prayer was probably no more than ten words, 'Lord Jesus, heal this headache and take away all pain.' I asked her how she felt.

"She rubbed the back of her neck and twisted her head from side to side. A huge smile erupted on her face as she exclaimed, 'It's better! The headache is completely gone!'

"You would think that having God do a miracle in the supermarket would jolt me out of my "ugly mode," but alas, it didn't. That is until I saw her little girl jump up and down like a pogo stick with excitement, chanting and singing, 'Mama is better! Mama is better!' Then I began to comprehend the stress and pain this woman had been experiencing.

"This little one skipped and danced through the store as she joyously helped fill the baskets with vegetables, fruit, cheese, meat, bread, milk, cereal, and healthy snacks for later. With the baskets filled and my list complete, we headed for the checkout. After paying for all the groceries, I left the store first.

"From my car, I waited and watched for them to come out. Soon they appeared and walked across the parking lot toward a large white van. Before they reached their destination, the van door slid open as a clatter of youthful activity spilled out into the snow. Now several children bounced up and down with excitement reaching into the overflowing bags.

"Finally, as I saw the unhindered joy and gratitude of the entire family, my heart melted. I was

> the least likely candidate,
>> the worst example of servitude,
>>> the poorest display of God's goodness,
>> the stingiest prospect of generosity,

226

the grumpiest host for His presence
and yet,

"God still used me to bring healing to a woman and provide for a family.

> *I can never claim the credit for anything God does through me.*

"Even on my best days, when I think I have it all together, I fall far short of what God desires. Why He chooses to use the frailness of humanity to display His presence is beyond understanding, but He does. He just needs someone, anyone, who is willing to be used."

I sat at the reception desk of a thriving manufacturing company. This Tuesday started like any normal morning. All the employees except for me were in a weekly safety meeting. No sooner had the meeting begun when two young salespeople entered, one male and one female.

Explaining to them that the manager would be busy for a while, I welcomed them to be seated until the meeting was over.

"It wasn't difficult to overhear their conversation. The young man had been in an accident twelve years ago. Ever since that time, chronic pain and restricted mobility had hindered him from doing many of the things he once enjoyed. They chatted for some time about the injury and his prognosis.

"I had witnessed God heal back injuries and knew that He could do it again. Listening to the young man's discouragement prompted me to speak. 'God doesn't heal every time I pray for people, but I have seen Him heal enough to know that He can and will. May I pray for you?' I asked.

"The salesman appeared more than a little shocked by my forthrightness, but hesitantly agreed. I said the shortest prayer asking God to heal every part of his spine and remove all pain. Then I asked him to test it out. He looked at me like I was bordering insanity, but stood up and cautiously tried a few movements. The surprised look on his face proved there was a change. He now had more mobility and less pain than just a few minutes before.

"Spurred on by the evidence of God's touch, I asked if I could pray again for him.

"With reluctance, He agreed. I briefly thanked God for what He had already done and offered another quick prayer. I was concerned workers would soon be rushing through the reception area and bring an end to what God was doing for this young man.

"When I asked him to test it again, he was obviously annoyed but rose to his feet muttering something to the effect that I was being pushy. If pushy was what it took to release a man from twelve years of pain, then pushy I would be. This time the pain was completely gone and he was able to bend down and touch his toes—something he wasn't able to do previously. For a full minute, he twisted his torso back and forth, and from side to side. He reached and stretched. Even though he was now pain-free and able to move unhindered, he remained almost unphased by the whole encounter.

"However, the young woman with him was ecstatic. Her eyes grew bigger with each prayer initiative. She knew she was witnessing a miracle. She had been his partner for long enough to know the extent of his injury and the limiting effects it had had on him. His restricted movements and the draining nature of chronic pain had previously hindered his ability to function normally.

"Though the young man never gave God credit for touching his back that day, the young woman left with her faith elevated."

One cannot separate the miraculous from the Word of God and maintain the integrity of the Bible. From the first words in Genesis to the closing chapter of Revelation, God is evidenced by His supernatural workings and power.

Jesus, the express image of the Invisible God, (Heb 1:3) **"was a man accredited by God to you by miracles, wonders and signs, which God did among you through him . . ."** (Acts 2:22). Don't miss the reality of this profound statement. As a man, not God, Jesus relied upon His Father to work through Him. But unlike us, He was a man fully yielded and obedient to God.

Jesus sent out His disciples, giving them authority and power to teach as He taught and do the works He had been doing. Astonishingly, He said they would do even greater works than His (Jn 14:12).

> **"He said to them, "Go into all the world and preach the gospel to all creation. Whoever believes and is baptized will be saved, but whoever does not believe will be condemned. And these signs will accompany those who believe: In my name *they will* drive out demons; *they will* speak in new tongues; *they will* pick up snakes with their hands; and when they drink deadly poison, it will not hurt them at all; *they will* place their hands on sick people, and they will get well . . . Then the disciples went out and preached everywhere, and *the Lord worked* with them, and confirmed his word by the signs that accompanied it."**
> **Mark 16:15-20**
> **(Emphasis Mine)**

Signs, wonders and miracles marked not just the lives of these apostles, but also many other faithful servants and followers of Christ. The writer of Hebrews affirms,

> **"This salvation, which was first announced by the Lord, was confirmed to us by those who heard him. God also testified to it by signs, wonders and**

229

**various miracles, and by the gifts of the Holy Spirit
distributed according to his will."
Hebrews 2:3-4**

*"The miraculous element in Christianity and the fact
that God can act in this world of ours is essential to
the vitality of Christianity. Without this aspect, prayer
becomes meaningless . . ."* [1]

God has not and will not change (Heb 13:8; Jas 1:17). In our day, in this generation, God is moving in an increasing measure through the same signs, wonders and miracles we read about within the pages of the Bible. He is calling ordinary women and men, boys and girls, young and old together, anointing them through the Holy Spirit to turn hearts to Himself. God has not suddenly become powerless and silent; signs and wonders continue to follow those who believe. The miraculous is the abundant fruit resulting from the seeds of prayer.

Despondency and neglect of faith followed those who **"refused to listen and failed to remember the miracles (God) performed among them"** (Neh 9:17). Continuously as I interviewed people of all ages, they joyfully remembered and shared God's grace and goodness witnessed through answered prayer, often in ways they least expected. Remembering

reignites the flames of our first love,

realigns us with the faithfulness of God,

redirects our focus to the Source of life,

rekindles the passion of His Presence,

restores the deep reservoir of faith,

re-energizes our desire to pray and to keep on praying. Remembering is critical to all vibrant faith.

We cannot and will not be silent about the good things God has done. He still sovereignly moves among us by His Spirit.

***

Notes
1. Bill Johnson and Randy Clark, *The Essential Guide to Healing: Equipping All Christians to Pray for the Sick* (Bloomington, Chosen Books, 2011), 88.

Epilogue

During John's revelation of Jesus Christ and view into Heaven, he saw an angel seemingly in charge of the prayers of the saints.

**"Another angel, who had a golden censer, came
and stood at the altar. He was given much incense
to offer, with the prayers of all God's people, on
the golden altar in front of the throne. The smoke
of the incense, together with the prayers of God's
people, went up before God from the angel's hand.
Then the angel took the censer, filled it with fire
from the altar, and hurled it on the earth, and
there came peals of thunder, rumblings,
flashes of lightning and an earthquake."**
Revelation 8:3-5

Prayer unites Heaven and Earth, the common with the holy, humanity with God.

Every prayer precious and treasured in Heaven.
Every prayer heard by God.
Every prayer mingled with Heaven's incense.
Every prayer empowered with authority.
Every prayer affecting earth.
No prayer too small or frail.
No prayer goes unheard.
No prayer ineffective or powerless.
No prayer untouched by Heaven.
Every prayer make a difference.

**"I will answer your cry for help every time
you pray, and you will find and feel my
presence even in your time of pressure
and trouble. I will be your glorious hero
and give you a feast. You will be satisfied
with a full life and with all that I do
for you. For you will enjoy the
fullness of my salvation!"**
Psalm 91:15-16

Be assured that **"every time you pray"** something shifts—something changes. So, pray! Pray on, warrior! Pray until Christ returns or until you are with Him in Heaven. Prayer is a grace gift to God's children, combining human initiative with God's directive, giving divinely inspired utterances with Heaven's authority, empowering the natural with the imprint of God's supernatural grace, mercy and love.

Acknowledgments

I would be gravely amiss to fail to acknowledge the dozens of voices echoing throughout the pages of *Unlocking Legacy*. You have so graciously opened the window for us to quietly and solemnly view your sacred times with God.

Through your triumphs and failures, you have gained and shared spiritual insight I neither possess nor can speak about. Your testimonies have deeply impacted my own prayer initiative, as I'm sure they will for those who read your stories. Your lives reveal that a praying lifestyle, though perceived as dead and powerless by many, remains vibrant and potently strong, crossing international boundaries. Young and old have picked up the mantle of prayer to carry it with power and authority. Daily battles are fought and won in the spirit realm because of your unseen prayer initiatives.

Souls are being saved,
lives are being transformed,
deliverances are being released,
healing anointing flows powerfully,
and justice is being executed.
How? On bended knees!

Just like your stories have ignited the flame of prayer in my life, so they shall in all who read *Unlocking Legacy*.

Because of your vulnerability and honest witness to the grace and power of God who hears and answers prayer, glory, honor, and praise resounds in the heavenly realm. God is the beginning; He is the initiator of prayer; He hears our faintest cry; He responds with love and wisdom. To Him belongs reverent thanks.

**"The LORD is righteous in all his ways
and faithful in all he does.
The LORD is near to all who call on him,
to all who call on him in truth."
Psalm 145:17-18**

Author Bio

In times of prayer, the Father whispers an invitation, "Come Little One. Listen to me."

His descriptive name fits the author well. "Little One!" Little in the shadow of awesome God. No other description is necessary— Little One.

Contact

https://maward.ca/about-maryann-ward/

ReMade Ministries
Box 205
Balgonie, Saskatchewan, CA
S0G 0E0

maryann@maward.ca

Other Books By

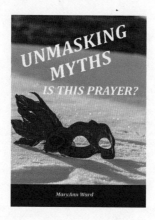

Unmasking Myths, the first book in a series on prayer, reveals the secrets to powerful effective prayer through multi-generational testimonies from around the world. The potential of prayer becomes clear! Discover the unmasked beauty and wonder of prayer within the pages of *Unmasking Myths.*
Published 2020.

Olivia & Me, a children's picture book, presenting the truth of John 10:10, **"I have to come that they may have life, and have it to the full."** Through a parallel journey between a little girl and a caterpillar turned butterfly, *Olivia & Me* illustrates life **"to the full."** On earth and in heaven.
Published 2017